# THE SPURS SHIRT

Published by Vision Sports Publishing Ltd in 2018

Vision Sports Publishing
19-23 High Street
Kingston upon Thames
Surrey
KT1 1LL
www.visionsp.co.uk

© Tottenham Hotspur Football Club
Text © Simon Shakeshaft
Shirt images © Daren Burney and Simon Shakeshaft
ISBN: 978-1909534-76-6

Authors: Simon Shakeshaft, Daren Burney and Neville Evans
Editor: Jim Drewett
Writer: Adam Powley
Art editor: Doug Cheeseman
Editorial production: Ed Davis
Shirt photography: Paul Downes/3Objectives Photography and Mansel Davies Photography
Kit illustrations: Daniel Gellatley
Shirt consultant: Liam Ridley
Historical consultants: Tony Sealey (kits) and Bob Goodwin
Club liaison: Jon Rayner and Gary Jacobson

This book is an officially licensed product

The views expressed in this book do not necessarily reflect the views, opinions or policies of Tottenham Hotspur Football and Athletic Co Ltd, nor those of any persons connected with the same.

Tottenham Hotspur Football and Athletic Co Ltd
Lilywhite House
782 High Road
London
N17 0BX
www.tottenhamhotspur.com

Printed and bound in Italy by L.E.G.O.

# THE SPURS SHIRT

## THE OFFICIAL HISTORY OF THE TOTTENHAM HOTSPUR JERSEY

By SIMON SHAKESHAFT, DAREN BURNEY & NEVILLE EVANS

F.A. CUP FINAL
WEMBLEY 1981

# CONTENTS

# FOREWORD

*By* LEDLEY KING

As a one-club man who played at Tottenham for my whole career, and who was privileged enough to be named captain, wearing the Spurs shirt was one of the greatest honours of my life.

I was, and still am, immensely proud that I got to wear that famous shirt so many times. I first did so as a youth team player. There were no names on the back in those days, but at least my teammates and I did not have to wear hand-me-downs like apprentices did in the past.

When I broke into the first team squad I was given the number 26. I didn't really think about the number – I was more concerned with playing well – but as I became a regular those two digits became more and more important to me. I liked the fact that there was a '6' in the number. That to me signifies a proper footballing defender. You might be surprised to know how much these little things actually mean to players.

How a player looks and feels in their shirt is important. At first I liked my shirts to be loose and baggy, but I look back on photographs of some of those early games and my shirt looks massive. I guess it was just the fashion at the time. If you feel good and comfortable you perform better. When skin-tight shirts were brought in that caused some laughs in the dressing room: those tight Kappa tops were very revealing and certainly forced a few people into the gym to get on the weights.

When I was playing we would always get to see the new season's shirts in pre-season and be asked our opinion on the fit and style, and of course there were some season's designs and colours we preferred more than others. I particularly liked the 2002/03 dark blue away shirt, but not so much the brown away shirt of 2006/07 – although even that one grew on me.

But to be honest if you are lucky enough to play for this great club then you grow to love every Tottenham shirt. I used to have a collection containing one each of my home and away shirts from every season, although they have started to drift away – mainly given to charities. Some of mine are also no doubt in the collections of some of my opponents. As a rule I never asked to swap shirts after a match because I saw it as a sign of weakness, but if I was asked I would swap so I've got a few. Having said that I did once ask Ryan Giggs when I was young but he said he wasn't allowed.

This superb book tells the story of the Spurs shirts worn over the decades by generations of Tottenham legends. It's not just the story of the shirts but the people who wore them, and the games they were featured in. In fact, leafing through the wonderful shirts on these pages, they tell the story of the club itself and really bring its history to life.

My story came to an end when I played my last game in Tottenham colours in my emotional and unforgettable testimonial in 2014. I'd stopped playing by then so I filled the shirt out a little more than I perhaps should have, but I was very proud to pull it on one last time. It's one of the shirts that I cherish.

With so many great players pulling on the lilywhite shirt before me, it was a dream as a young kid to do the same and it means so much to me that my dream came true. It always will.

Enjoy the book!

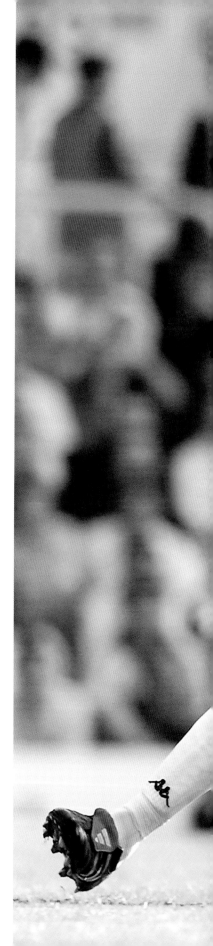

# LILYWHITE & BLUE

There is nothing that identifies a football club more than its colours. Players and managers come and go, but along with the home ground, the shirt and the club crest that adorns it are the pillars on which the identity of every football club are built.

No matter how much styles change and designs alter – arguably not always for the best – the shirt represents the history and heritage of the team that wears it, and the pure lilywhite and blue of Tottenham Hotspur Football Club is one of the most famous and iconic football jerseys of them all.

This book presents the greatest collection of Spurs match worn shirts ever seen in one place. All of the 150 plus shirts (worn by more than 110 different players) featured on these pages are match worn by – or at least prepared for the use of – Spurs legends, stalwarts or cult heroes who have pulled on the lilywhite jersey over the course of the rich history of the club.

The rarity and value of the shirts in this book cannot be overstated. Plotting a course through time, they literally have drops of blood, beads of sweat and tears seeped into their very fabric, so providing a unique and tangible gateway into the history and heritage of the famous London club.

Each shirt featured on the following 300 or so pages conjures up memories and moments from Tottenham Hotspur's glorious past – from Danny Blanchflower lifting the FA Cup in 1961 to Jurgen Klinsmann's debut goal and

*Right: The modern incarnation of the famous Spurs jersey – match prepared for Harry Kane – hangs in the dressing room, ready for action*

*Far right: Tottenham Hotspur legend Steve Perryman is pictured in the pure lilywhite kit of the 1970s. For many this is the classic Spurs shirt*

"THE PROUD COCKEREL, THE CREW-NECK, THE PURE LILYWHITE. WEARING IT YOU FELT LIKE YOU COULD BEAT ANYONE" STEVE PERRYMAN

## "I WOULD HAVE PLAYED FOR NOTHING JUST TO HAVE BEEN ABLE TO PULL ON THAT SHIRT WITH THE COCKEREL CREST"
### ALAN GILZEAN

*Above: Umbro supplied Spurs from the mid 1930s until 1977, producing some of the club's cleanest and best-loved jerseys, including the short-sleeved style worn by the 1961 Double team and the long-sleeved, crew-necked shirt sported by Alan Gilzean (above, right) in 1966*

*Right: The late 1970s saw a revolution at White Hart Lane, with the arrival of Argentinian World Cup stars Ricky Villa and Ossie Ardiles and drastically different new kits from Admiral*

*Far right: In 2017 Tottenham Hotspur entered into a new kit supply arrangement with Nike, and the first shirts produced by the dynamic global brand were clean, smart and classically Spurs*

dive celebration or Gareth Bale's one-man demolition of Inter Milan in the Champions League. Gaze at Ricky Villa's No.5 shirt from the 1981 FA Cup final and the memories of that mazy run through the Manchester City defence come flooding back, and you can almost hear the Wembley roar as the Argentinian slides the ball under City keeper Joe Corrigan to seal victory.

The lilywhite shirt with the navy cockerel is an instantly recognisable expression of Tottenham Hotspur's heart and soul. It is so much more than a few yards of fabric and thread. As the great Steve Perryman says: "The proud cockerel, the crew-neck, the pure lilywhite. The shirt was clean, it was proper and it stood out. It made you think of the legends who have worn that shirt with pride before you. When you were wearing it you felt you could achieve anything. We could beat anyone."

Spurs have used 11 different kit suppliers over the last 100 years or so, including all the major manufacturers – Umbro, Bukta, Puma, adidas and Nike – allowing them to be at the forefront of groundbreaking and cutting-edge football kit development and reveal brave and bold designs from the likes of Admiral, Hummel, Kappa and Under Armour.

Supporters of course will have their favourite shirts and ones that mean most to them. Specific shirts and certain numbers will evoke memories of different Spurs teams and players – Chivers 9, Hoddle 10, Gascoigne 8, King 26 and Bale 11. With an example of virtually every shirt from the modern era, *The Spurs Shirt* brings those memories back to life by lifting the older shirts out of the black and white photographs as well as cataloguing every variation of trim, stripe, hoop, half brace, chevron and sash on the multitude of more recent styles and colours.

For the players who wore it, the shirt was special too. As the original King of White Hart Lane, Alan Gilzean, once said: "In the end I would have played for nothing just to have been able to pull on that white shirt with the cockerel on it."

The Spurs shirt is not just another white shirt. Some football jerseys are defined by their colour scheme or a distinctive crest. In the case of Spurs – one of the first clubs to wear a club crest on its shirt for every match, not just showpiece occasions – it is a combination of both. It comes attached with a myriad of myths and legends, all of which have been painstakingly researched for this book so that the truth can be categorically revealed. Were Spurs really influenced by the colours of the once mighty Preston North End when they chose white shirts and navy shorts in the 1890s? Is it true that manager Bill Nicholson was copying the great

Real Madrid side of the late 1950s and early 1960s when he sent the team out to play their first European campaign in 1961 wearing white shorts, starting a tradition that is still upheld today? Was the 1987 FA Cup final mix-up, when half of the shirts did not have the logo of sponsor Holsten on the front, really a publicity stunt? The folklore is all part of the allure.

*The Spurs Shirt* is a commitment to the preservation and protection of the famous Spurs colours. Match worn shirts have become the pinnacle of football memorabilia collecting, and with the assistance of a group of collectors without whom it would not have been possible, this is a project that hasn't been done before, certainly not to the level of detail that the subject matter deserves.

So, sit back and indulge yourself in the traditions and colours that are etched forever into the rich tapestry that is the history of Tottenham Hotspur Football Club.

# THE EVOLUTION
# OF THE SHIRT
## 1882-1960

# THE EVOLUTION OF THE SHIRT

*Above: The cover of the 1908 club history in which the first ever reference to the Spurs colours appears*

*Previous pages: Andy Duncan, Albert Hall and Willie Hall take a break to admire their newly numbered shirts at the Lane in September 1939*

Considering the importance of the kit to the culture and identity of football clubs, and in the context of the microscopic media coverage of modern football, it seems unbelievable that we have no idea what colour shirt the first Hotspur team played in. But in the early days of Victorian football, when new clubs were sprouting up all over England, no one could have known how big the game, and the clubs themselves, would become or how central to their identities their colours would come to be.

So when, in 1882, schoolboy members of Hotspur Cricket Club looking to play sport in the winter months formed a football team, no one had the foresight to record what colours they wore in the friendly matches played in their inaugural season. However, in keeping with many of the clubs formed at the time, it is possible that the playing kit would have been influenced by the school colours from one or more of the two main schools which the Hotspur Football Club players attended – St John's Middle Class School and Tottenham Grammar School. But we have no idea what these colours were. Like all clubs formed at this time when the first roots of the game were starting to grow, Hotspur FC were playing for fun. Not only would its young members have had little access to funds for football playing kit, the outfits the players wore would most likely have been adapted school sports kit, converted dresswear or literally whatever was available. In fact, it is likely that in those very first matches the team would have played in a mishmash of shirt styles of various colours and shades.

One very significant fact can be gleaned, however, from the club's first accounts book from 1882, which recorded the player subscriptions and the club's expenses. There is no mention of any playing kit, but the fact that the club purchased a set of wooden goalposts, flagpoles and white paint is recorded. More importantly, it is noted that posts – which would have been transported to each fixture (at this time there were no crossbars) – were painted blue and white.

The first historical reference to the Hotspur team colours appears in the 1908 history of the club, *The White Hart: Souvenir of The Spurs Entry to The English League*, which states that at the club's first AGM in August 1883 it was recorded that: "The colours were dark blue jersey, white breeches, dark blue stockings and cap."

A later history book, *A Romance of Football: The History of the Tottenham Hotspur FC*, printed in 1921, gives further

*Above: A graphical representation of the evolution of the Spurs kit which includes black and white photographs of some of the early kits which have been colourised, including the very first strip which is wrongly pictured featuring navy shorts*

detail from the 1883 AGM, quoting a rule which stated: "That the uniform of the club be navy blue, with scarlet shield on left side of jersey with the letter 'H' thereon, and that every member is requested to wear same in matches".

The 'H' on the scarlet shield, of course stood for 'Hotspur', the name inherited from the cricket club from which the football club was spawned that was inspired by the swashbuckling medieval hero Sir Henry Percy, eldest son of the Earl of Northumberland who owned land in the Tottenham area. The colour of the shield on which the 'H' sat may come as a surprise to some, but red had no significance to the club at this time and indeed would go on to feature even more prominently as the team's strip underwent numerous changes during the pioneering Victorian years.

IN AUGUST 1883 IT WAS RECORDED THAT "THE COLOURS WERE DARK BLUE JERSEY, WHITE BREECHES, DARK BLUE STOCKINGS AND CAP"

In the absence of any photographic evidence, exactly what this first Spurs shirt looked like can only be speculated upon. The players would almost certainly have purchased their own navy flannel shirts or heavy woolen jumpers from an everyday men's outfitters, but the shape of the shield or style of the letter 'H' is unknown. Equally we do not know if the crests were supplied by the club or, more likely, made and sewn on at home making each one unique.

The mention of caps in the 1908 history indicates that at least some of the players wore caps during the 1883/84 season. Caps would have been a fairly common sight on early Victorian footballers but were becoming less popular by the 1880s and it seems that it wasn't something that the young Hotspurs persisted with.

Whatever the exact form it took, this first recorded kit did not hang around for long as Hotspur FC moved with the game's rapidly changing times, and in fact it would change at least five times in the next 15 years before the famous club colours that we associate Spurs with today were finally adopted.

There is conflicting historical evidence as to the next stage in the history of the Spurs shirt. At some point the red shield emblem was dropped and replaced by the letters 'HFC' stitched across the navy shirt, and it is generally believed that this was for the 1884/85 season before a switch to a completely new kit for the following campaign. However, there is some evidence that the latter change may actually have happened sooner.

What we do know is that at a meeting held on 2 April 1884 the club adopted a new name, Tottenham Hotspur FC, in order to avoid confusion with another London club

also called Hotspur. This was some four days after the 1884 English (FA) Cup final which some of the boys had attended. According to the 1908 history book, the Spurs players were so impressed with Blackburn Rovers that they decided to adopt the cup winners' kit for the following season. Rovers were emerging as a leading force in the game and they would go on to record three consecutive FA Cup triumphs in 1884, '85 and '86 (the first two against Queen's Park). The 1908 book states: "By advice of Mr Bailey we scratched our match and went to the Oval and saw Blackburn Rovers beat Queen's Park, a match none of us will ever forget, especially Jemmy Brown's tussles with Chas. Campbell and Dr John Smith's centre forward play... The next season [1884/85] saw us change our colours and adopt the half blue and half white colours of the Rovers."

However, the 1921 version of the club's early history tells the story differently. It claims that the Spurs players cancelled their final game of the season, on 4 April 1885, and travelled to the Oval to see Rovers lift the second of their trio of FA Cups. The book goes on to state that the club adopted Rovers' shirt colours for the start of the 1885/86 season; in other words, one season later: "Disdaining the old blue jerseys which had 'HFC' stitched across their front and thus made the players appear like fishermen, the Spurs changed their colours in favour of those of their much-admired team, Blackburn Rovers, viz, half light blue and half white with the letter 'H' near the shoulder."

With Rovers playing consecutive cup finals in 1884 and 1885, both against Queen's Park, it is easy to understand how confusion may have arisen. However, the 1908 version appears to be more plausible, specifically referring to the Queen's Park player Dr John Smith who only played in the

THE SPURS PLAYERS WERE SO IMPRESSED WITH BLACKBURN ROVERS THAT THEY DECIDED TO ADOPT THE CUP WINNERS' KIT

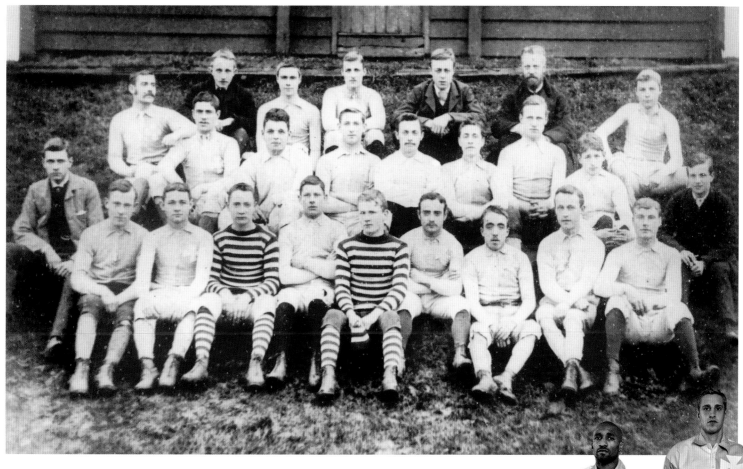

earlier final, and it seems more likely that "disdaining the old blue jerseys which had 'HFC' stitched across their front" would have coincided with the change of name (which would have rendered the 'HFC' inaccurate) in 1884. And it is quite possible that a combination of both the scarlet 'H' shield and the HFC lettered shirts could have been worn during the 1883/84 season, as it was common practice for teams to wear a mishmash of kits at the time.

Another source of some historical confusion is the badge worn on the smart new light-blue-and-white-halved shirts. For whilst the 1921 history refers to an 'H' symbol, the first known photograph of a Tottenham Hotspur team, from the 1885/86 season, shows the players wearing shirts featuring a style of Christian cross, similar to a Maltese cross, actually known as a croix pattée. It would appear that both variations were worn at some point.

The reason why the letter 'H' was again chosen is obvious, but precisely why the Spurs players chose the croix pattée as an emblem is not known. However, it was common for the new Victorian teams to adopt such symbols. Indeed, Blackburn Rovers themselves had originally sported this Christian motif on their jersey, the design originating from the Shrewsbury public school which a significant number of the founding Rovers players had attended. And the Manchester team Gorton, who would go on to become Manchester City, used exactly the same croix pattée design on their favoured black shirts at more or less the same time as the newly christened Tottenham Hotspur.

*Above: The Spurs team pictured during the 1894/95 season, a period during which the club was nicknamed 'The Tottenham Reds'*

*Below: Some of the key landmarks in the evolution of the Spurs shirt*

identifies the year although the 1921 book mistakenly states that it is from the 1884/85 season). In one of two grainy team pictures from the occasion, two players can be seen wearing woolen, hooped tops with crew-necks and matching stockings, which may be photographic evidence of the mixed make-up of the team's strip from that era.

Because of all the conflicting historical evidence, then, we cannot be certain exactly which season the blue-and-white-halved shirts were first worn, and with which emblem. The 1908 history suggests that the 'H' jerseys were worn during the 1884/85 season. But with the club becoming established as Tottenham Hotspur the single letter symbol was dropped in favour of the cross symbol for the 1885/86 season. The 1921 history claims that the 'H' was chosen for the 1885/86 season, although if this is true then by October when the first photographs were taken – only three games into the season – it had changed to the cross.

There is of course the possibility that both symbols were worn during the 1885/86 season, with the navy HFC 'fishermen's jerseys' used throughout the preceding 1884/85 campaign.

It's true that the emblem had religious significance – indeed this design of cross could well have been used as a symbol by St John's, the local school which some of the young Spurs players attended. But the likelihood is that the cross was chosen for its design aesthetic rather than any religious meaning.

The blue and white jerseys featuring the croix pattée emblem were worn by the majority of the players in the first known photographs of a Tottenham Hotspur team which are believed to have been taken before the club's first competitive match, a London Association Cup tie against St Albans FC on 17 October 1885 (the 1908 history correctly

After 1886 it is not known what colours the team wore over the next three years until the 1889/90 season, when records reveal that navy blue and white was now the club's colour scheme of choice, with the shirt believed to have featured navy and white stripes. This soon gave way, in 1890, to a significant alteration to the Spurs shirt palette that would be unthinkable today – red shirts with navy shorts, or 'knickers' as they were described in that era.

1883/84     1884/85     1890–95     1895–98     1898–1906

# ACCORDING TO EARLY HISTORY BOOKS, AROUND 1892 THE CLUB EARNED THE NICKNAME 'THE TOTTENHAM REDS'

With Woolwich Arsenal's move from south to north London still more than 20 years away, there was nothing contentious about the colour red at this time. Red was a popular choice for football teams because it was available as one of the three common colours sold by outfitters, along with white and blue. Club colours were not yet woven into the fabric of football teams' identities and were therefore not sacrosanct to their supporters. Indeed, in 1886 Spurs moved their office into a building on the High Road called the 'Red House' and, according to early history books, around 1892 the club earned the nicknamed the 'Tottenham Reds'.

Red shirts, then, were worn for six seasons as the club grew in stature and appeal. The quality of the players improved as well. Star player Jack Jull was called up to represent Middlesex, becoming the first Spurs player to gain representative honours. In the team photograph from the 1894/95 season, Jull is pictured with the Middlesex FA crest proudly sewn on to his red Spurs shirt, which was a common practice at the time.

With Spurs still using red shirts as their first choice during the 1895/96 season, on 26 October 1895 the team ran out on to its Northumberland Park pitch to play the Royal Artillery in chocolate-and-caramel-striped shirts. These exotic colours were chosen because it had been expected that the soldiers would wear red, making this the club's first official alternative shirt. The eye-catching style, described in a press report as "Chocolate and Yellow", must have proved popular because it became the regular first choice for the next two years. Then in 1898, with the club just 16 years old and still forging its identity and place in the game and the community, Tottenham Hotspur adopted the famous shirt colour that it is synonymous with today.

The widely accepted reason for the switch to white shirts and navy shorts is that Spurs were once again emulating a successful team, this time Preston North End. This is a myth. The fact of the matter is without doubt far less romantic.

In December 1895, following the Payne's Boot Affair – when Spurs were punished by the FA for breaking the 'amateur' rules by purchasing a pair of boots for new signing Ernie Payne – Tottenham Hotspur turned professional. The consequence of this is that the club was now allowed to purchase playing kit for its players. Previously it would have been against the rules. Then in 1898, Tottenham Hotspur Football Club – now playing in the higher level of the Southern League – became a limited company, so whilst not awash with money there was enough in the pot for the club to consider purchasing a team strip rather than relying on players to bring their own.

The question was what shirts should the club buy? Spurs had changed their strip so many times in their first 16 years that there was no strong affinity with any one colour. White was almost certainly chosen for practical rather than sporting reasons. Firstly because it was easily available, and secondly because at the time no other team

*Above: The navy-and-white-striped shirts worn by Spurs during the 1889/90 season*

*Below: First worn as a change strip, chocolate and caramel stripes were adopted as the first-choice colours from 1896 to 1898*

*One of the earliest known photographs of Spurs wearing their now familiar white and blue colours, taken in 1898*

## THERE IS NO EVIDENCE TO SUGGEST THAT SPURS CHOSE WHITE SHIRTS AND NAVY SHORTS AS A TRIBUTE TO PRESTON NORTH END

in the league had white shirts registered as its first choice. As a report on the new colour scheme in the *Weekly Herald* on 15 July 1898 explained: "No other club in the Southern League is similarly equipped". This would of course mean a reduction in the number of occasions when Spurs would require an alternative strip. The choice of white, therefore, was very much a common sense decision.

There is no primary evidence whatsoever to suggest that Spurs chose white shirts and blue shorts as a tribute to Preston North End. For whilst it's true that Preston had become famous for their dominance of the early Football League, and in particular their unbeaten 'Invincible' season of 1888/89 when they became the first English team to do the league and FA Cup 'Double', by the time Spurs adopted their colours Preston were actually a team on the wane, with their historic achievements having taken place a decade previously.

What has generally become an accepted fact, passed down from one history book to another, appears to originate from the 1921 history which states: "About this time the club colours were changed to white shirts and blue knickers. This was a compliment to Preston N.E., who were then one of the best teams in the country". The source of this 'fact' is not stated, but may well come from the same 15 July report in the *Weekly Herald* which included the sentence: "The Spurs will this year wear the famous Preston North End colours, viz, snow white shirts and

navy blue knickers." But there is no mention here of Spurs' new choice of colours being *inspired* by the exploits of Preston some 10 years earlier. The newspaper was simply stating the fact that its local team would be playing the forthcoming season in the colour scheme that Preston were – at that time – the most famous club to wear. It would appear that the writer of the 1921 history has made an assumption whilst looking to find a reason for the colour change similar to that which led the club to emulate Blackburn Rovers in the mid 1880s. And once printed in an official history in black and white, the myth was repeated and perpetuated over time until it became 'fact'.

With the club now supplying match shirts to its players in order to give the team a neater and more uniform appearance, the new look Spurs ran out against Bedminster for the opening league game of the 1898/99 season looking resplendent in their new attire.

Then, three years after the decision to switch to white shirts and blue shorts, the sensational 1901 FA Cup final triumph against Sheffield United catapulted the club to national fame as the first (and still the only) non-league team to win the famous trophy. The ensuing newspaper and newsreel coverage of the historic win captured the imagination of the nation and the football world beyond, sealing lilywhite and navy as the colours that would go on to be forever associated with Tottenham Hotspur.

By now, both the traditional clothing factories and a small number of new sport-specific shirt manufacturers – two of the best-known being Bukta, established in Stockport in 1879 as Edward Buck & Sons and suppliers of kit to Nottingham Forest in 1884, and William Shillcock of Birmingham – were producing jerseys

S.T.DADD.

especially for team sports. These more robust, football-specific cotton woven shirts would have been produced in various weights and differed from the traditional Victorian dress shirts that they replaced by having a fold-down collar. The older style flannel or flannelette dress shirts would have generally had high or detachable collars.

We don't know which company manufactured Tottenham's playing kit in the early 1900s but an insight into how homespun the early football shirt industry can be

*Above and left: The 1901 FA Cup final triumph made the name Tottenham Hotspur, and their lilywhite shirts and navy shorts, famous the world over*

*Above: King George V inspects the Tottenham Hotspur players – wearing a cockerel crest on their shirts for the first time – before the 1921 FA Cup final against Wolverhampton Wanderers*

*Right: The Stamford Bridge pitch was so muddy that the Spurs team had changed into a new set of shirts – without cockerel crests – before lifting the trophy*

gleaned from the fact that between 1907 and 1911 the club was supplied by a local outfitter, HR Brookes, of 778 Seven Sisters Road, which was about a mile up from White Hart Lane, the ground into which Spurs had moved in 1899.

In the tough years immediately before and following the First World War, Spurs wore various forms of white shirts, usually with a collar and buttons and also occasionally with lace-up collars. As was common with all clubs at the time, the players' shirts did not carry a badge or club crest. These would only adorn teams' shirts for an appearance in the FA Cup final, by far and away the most prestigious match in football at the time. Which is why, when Spurs reached their second final in 1921, one of the most famous and

identifiable of all club crests appeared on the Tottenham Hotspur jersey for the first time.

By now the cockerel had been associated with Spurs for some time, because spurs were worn by fighting cockerels, and it had first appeared in printed material relating to the club in 1900. In 1909 it officially became the shining symbol of Spurs when – cast in the form of a 9ft copper statue – a cockerel was affixed to the top of the then new West Stand at White Hart Lane. Obviously then, when a shirt badge was required for the 1921 final 12 years later, the emblem chosen was a proud navy cockerel, mounted on a shield although not at this stage perched on a football (unlike the statue).

The final itself, against Wolverhampton Wanderers, was played in horrendously wet conditions at Stamford Bridge, so much so that the Spurs players (as did their opponents) changed into clean, dry shirts without crests for the second half. The *Guardian* newspaper reported: "The rain had ceased when the second half began, and a change into dry clothes had its effect on the Spurs players." Tottenham Hotspur won the match 1-0, and subsequently – in a break with the generally accepted tradition of only wearing their badge as a one-off for the cup final – chose to continue adorning their match shirts with the new club crest for the following and all subsequent seasons. This set an early precedent, and Spurs became one of the first major football clubs to feature its crest on the players' shirts for every match, a practice that for some teams did not become the norm until the early 1970s, some 50 years later.

It is not known which manufacturer supplied the Spurs shirts between 1911 and 1921, but it is believed that Spurs wore Bukta shirts for the 1921 final as in later years the company advertised the fact that they had supplied all the FA Cup final teams in the 1920s in their marketing material. And photographic evidence does confirm that Spurs were definitely wearing Bukta shirts between 1921 and 1924.

The manufacturer of the Spurs shirt between 1924 and 1935 is not known but following the addition of the cockerel crest in 1921 the style remained virtually unchanged for many years, save for the odd occasion when a set of badgeless shirts was worn, or a set without collars or buttons was obtained. There was a slight change in style in 1930 with a relatively brief experiment with cashmere – a material usually associated with luxurious fashion rather

## SPURS BECAME THE FIRST MAJOR FOOTBALL CLUB TO WEAR THE CLUB CREST ON THEIR SHIRTS FOR EVERY MATCH

than the demanding rough-and-tumble of football – which is known to have been used for the home shirt for a short spell in the first half of the 1930/31 season and even more briefly in 1933/34. These stylish shirts were considered a luxury, an indication of the stature of a club by now known to do things with a touch of class and style, but they were already a slightly off-white due to the material used. With cashmere retaining dirt and being difficult to launder it was impossible to maintain the all-important pure lilywhite look and as a consequence their lifespan as a Spurs shirt was brief. This style of shirt also saw the introduction of a sleeker cockerel crest design.

*Above: A signed photo of club legend Jimmy Dimmock shows the first incarnation of the cockerel crest*

*Below: In 1930 there was a flirtation with cashmere jerseys, here modelled by (from left to right) Eugene 'Taffy' O'Callaghan, Edward 'Ted' Harper and George Cook*

It was later in this decade that a new name enters the story of the Tottenham Hotspur shirt, one which would go on to enjoy a long and successful partnership with the club. Umbro was originally set up in Wilmslow, Cheshire, in 1924 as Humphreys Brothers Clothing by Harold Humphreys with his brother Wallace – hence 'Um' combined with 'Bro' – but they came to prominence as a major player in the 1930s and supplied shirts to a number of the FA Cup finalists, including Manchester City in 1934. Although shirt design was unchanged, Umbro's football jerseys were made from a knitted shrink-resistant cotton which they branded 'Tangeru', and they were quickly adopted by numerous clubs. This rapid rise pitched them directly against Bukta and the rivalry between the two Manchester-based companies was akin to the standing of Nike and adidas today.

Tottenham Hotspur jumped aboard the Umbro bandwagon during the second half of the 1935/36 season, adopting the manufacturer's 'Self Association' design ('Self' being the catalogue name for shirts of all one colour and 'Association' referring to the fact that they were designed for association football) football jersey in white as its home choice. It was the start of a relationship that would span – with some brief exceptions – the next 40 or so years.

Following the resumption of peacetime football after the Second World War, 1945/46 saw Spurs playing in the Football League South, before the Football League proper restarted in 1946/47. Spurs were then in the Second Division and initially, amid the strictures of post-war rationing, played in plain white shirts probably not made by Umbro and without a cockerel crest.

The crest had reappeared, along with a new set of shirts, by the April of that season, and towards the end of the decade short-sleeved versions more suitable for warmer weather were worn. Indeed, the earliest known surviving match worn Spurs shirt is a short-sleeved unbranded home shirt that originates from the collection of Ron Burgess, the legendary captain of Arthur Rowe's 1951 'Push and Run' title-winners.

The exact season or seasons when this historic shirt was worn is impossible to determine for certain, but it is believed to originate from the late 1940s. Why Burgess had it, who it was worn by and when is also a mystery, since the iconic Spurs skipper was more usually associated with the No.6. Unusually the shirt has a pocket with a variant of the

Far left: The oldest known surviving Spurs shirt, which belonged to club legend Ron Burgess and is believed to originate from the late 1940s

Left: Ron Burgess is pictured in the more common style of jersey from the late 1940s and early 1950s, with a more familiar style of club crest

standard club crest, and there is no branding. It also does not have a 'CC41' (Control Commodity rationing label) which you would expect on a jersey from this time which could mean that it actually originates from abroad, perhaps a foreign tour or friendly. Then it may have become a training shirt. Interestingly, the jersey has a very slight pink hue to it, which might be the result of it being washed in the same machine as the club's red change shirts worn between 1947 and 1949 and therefore potentially dating it to those years. Ultimately the true story of this mysterious shirt is lost in the mists of time.

It wasn't until 1955 that the Spurs shirt saw any significant change, when the club adopted the new style of 'Self Association with a V-Insert collar' Umbro shirts – still made from the Tangeru fabric – which featured a modern-looking collar. This collar only appeared on short-sleeved shirts and was worn by Spurs in the early part of the 1955/56 season. When it got colder the team reverted to wearing the previous style of long-sleeved button-collar jerseys. This combining of styles continued but with less and less frequent use of the long-sleeved shirts until the end of the 1957/58 season, by which time only the short-sleeved v-insert style was being worn.

Aston Villa are often credited with being the club that first wore shirts featuring a v-insert collar in 1969, some 13 years after Spurs and other clubs had started wearing this style of jersey. It seems that because the v-insert was small and non-contrasting in colour (i.e. the same colour as the rest of the shirt) it went somewhat unnoticed. The v-insert-style of collar became extremely popular in the early 1970s.

The No.9 shirt of this vintage featured here was worn by the 1951 title-winning centre forward Len Duquemin, and is another special and incredibly rare match worn Spurs shirt. It also features the new, thinner cockerel on the badge, and the cloth No.9 on the back of the shirt is mounted on a large white patch.

The v-insert Spurs shirt saw service up until 1959, when the v-neck style made famous and forever popular by the

## IT WASN'T UNTIL 1955 THAT THE SPURS SHIRT SAW ANY SIGNIFICANT CHANGE, WHEN THE CLUB ADOPTED A V-INSERT COLLAR

1961 Double team became the home shirt style. However, in 1956 there was a lesser-known foray into experimental football shirt design when a revolutionary shirt was used in floodlit matches which was specifically intended to make the players more visible under those conditions. Made from a man-made silk-like material called Rayon, these shirts were shiny and reflective and were worn with navy – or sometimes white – shorts made from the same material. Interestingly, navy Rayon (or another man-made fabric) shorts had been worn by the team since 1951.

This unusual home kit was used for floodlit games between September and December 1956. It saw action in the Anglo-Scottish Cup competition as well as in friendlies against Red Banner MTK from Hungary and – the first time it was worn – versus Racing Club de Paris. But whilst the shirts may have offered some visual benefits, any positives were negated by the fact that the material absorbed moisture and retained heat, therefore becoming very heavy, hot and uncomfortable. For this reason the experiment was short-lived. It is not known for certain which company manufactured these shirts, but many clubs experimented with the fabric at the time and a number of London clubs, including Fulham, used Rayon shirts produced by a London-based sportswear brand called Uwin.

There was also a little-known alternative 'amber' version of the Rayon shirt – described by former player Ricky George as "more of a gold colour, really" – which was first worn in 1958 and saw action in three floodlit games, against Finchley in the London Senior Cup and then against the touring opposition of Bela Vista of Brazil and Bucharest of Romania. This striking kit was worn with matching amber Rayon shorts.

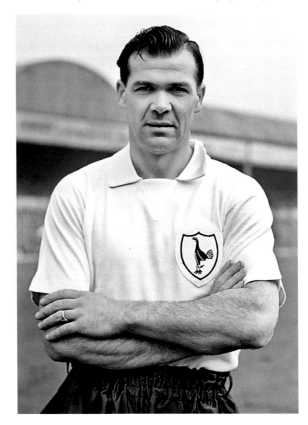

*Far right: An incredibly rare match worn Len Duquemin 'v-insert' shirt from the mid 1950s*

*Right: Duquemin is pictured wearing the same style of shirt prior to the FA Cup semi-final against Man City at Villa Park in March 1956*

*Above: In the 1950s and for the next couple of decades sportswear provision was dominated by local family retail shops. Spurs were supplied by Geo. Elsey & Son who had shops in Tottenham, Chiswick and Palmers Green*

# ALL CHANGE PLEASE

*Above: Ron Burgess is pictured wearing the style of change shirt that Spurs wore between 1952 and 1958*

*Below: Spurs (in the hoops) take on a Berlin XI at a snowy White Hart Lane in January 1901. The hoops are believed to have been red and blue*

The concept of the 'away' shirt is one we are familiar with today but the term did not formally arrive until the 1970s, although so-called alternative or change kits had been required by clubs since the early foundations of the Football League.

We have already covered the first recorded example of Spurs changing colours to avert a clash with the opposition, the 1895 match against the Royal Artillery, and the former 'home' chocolate-and-caramel-striped shirt was again called into action as a change jersey against Newton Heath (the precursor to Manchester United) in the FA Cup in 1899, while it is recorded that blue-and-white-striped shirts were worn between 1901 and 1911. Research has also shown that for a friendly against a Berlin XI, on a snowbound pitch at White Hart Lane in January 1901, Spurs wore light and dark broad-hooped crew-necked woolen jerseys. Using an orthochromatic chart to study black and white photographs of the match, it has been determined that the hoops were in all probability red and mid-blue. Early in 1908/09, red and white stripes were worn by Spurs against Fulham and Bolton Wanderers.

Change shirts worn by the club in the first half of the 1920s varied from a navy-blue-and-white-striped jersey with a laced collar, as worn in the 1920/21 season against Bolton, to a plain red shirt worn for the 1921 FA Cup semi-final against Preston, who wore blue. At this time, in the

event of a clash of colours in the FA Cup it was deemed that both teams must change. Drawing Preston – who this time chose red – again forced another change for the 1922 FA Cup semi-final at Hillsborough, with Spurs wearing blue and white vertical stripes, with the blue a slightly lighter shade than their shorts, most probably a consequence of the laundry which often gave shirts a very washed out look by this late stage of the season.

The earliest record of navy blue and white hoops being worn is during the 1925/26 season in a friendly against Real Madrid, and with slight variations in the size of the hoops this design became the mainstay of the change shirt until 1947. But the alternative shirt timeline is dotted with a number of 'one-offs' that today would be deemed a third shirt.

These one-off shirts included a red-and-white-striped shirt, worn in January 1931 (once again against Preston); a sky blue shirt surprisingly used for an away league game at Bury during the 1932/33 season; and red jerseys, which made a reappearance for the FA Cup loss to Luton that same season. It appears that none of these one-off shirts carried a cockerel crest.

Red then made two further appearances during the decade when it was worn in the early spring of 1937 for matches against Swansea and then against Spurs' regular kit antagonists, Preston. Even though the rivalry with

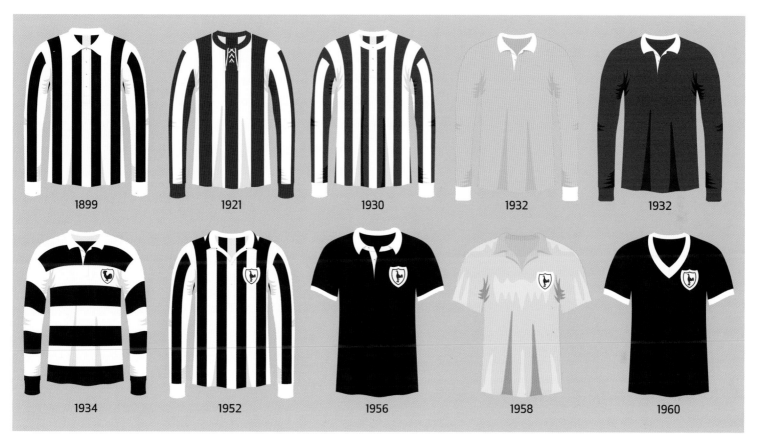

1899  1921  1930  1932  1932

1934  1952  1956  1958  1960

Arsenal – who arrived on Tottenham Hotspur's turf in 1913 and then took Spurs' Division One place in 1919 – was by this time very much part of the club's culture, red was still acceptable as an alternative colour. In fact, it returned to action on a Spurs away shirt as late as 1947, almost certainly because with post-war rationing the choice of colours would have been limited. These final red shirts were worn until 1949, the last time the colour was used as the primary colour on a Tottenham Hotspur outfield jersey – although it was used at times for goalkeepers' shirts up until the 1980s. It should be noted, however, that Arsenal regularly used white as an away colour until the mid 1960s.

In 1949, the club's away jerseys reverted to navy blue. This was the first time the popular colour of solid navy had been used for the Spurs jersey for 65 years, going back to the time when the club was still called Hotspur. Then for six seasons between 1952 and 1958, navy and white stripes returned, although full navy with white trim was also used

as another alternative for two seasons between 1956 and 1958. In 1959/60, plain navy shirts were introduced with a non-contrasting collar and cuffs rather than a white trim. There was also a brief foray into gold, with a cotton version of the experimental amber Rayon kit making an appearance for two games in 1959/60. But by the time Spurs embarked on the so-called modern era and the greatest period of their history to date, the highly popular – and now considered classically Spurs – navy shirt with white trim was to become the established away shirt.

It had been quite a journey to get to this point, with a multitude of colours and combinations, styles and materials worn over the first 80 years or so of the club's home and away shirt history. But as we enter the modern era, from which there are many more surviving match worn examples, the shirts contained in the main chapters of this book provide a unique perspective on the illustrious history of one of the world's great football clubs.

*Above: A graphical representation of some of Tottenham Hotspur's early alternative shirts, up to and including the classic 1960 jersey worn by the Double-winning team*

# THE COCKEREL CROWS
## 1960–1977

UMBRO & BUKTA

# FA CUP FINAL 1961

*Match worn by* PETER BAKER

With its clean, white simplicity, the lilywhite jersey worn by Bill Nicholson's glorious Double-winning heroes is one of *the* classic Spurs shirts.

Manufactured by Umbro, whose 'Choice of Champions' marketing strapline would soon come spectacularly true, the pure white, short-sleeved shirt was made from a lightweight cotton and featured a simple, thick v-neck collar and cuffs. This was the trend at the time, when most club shirts were derived from a limited number of template designs, and this particular style was described as the 'Continental Soccer Jersey' (later renamed the 'International Soccer Jersey') in Umbro's catalogue. There were different variations of the style, with the all-white version used by Spurs labelled 'Association Self' – 'Self' referring to the fact that it was all one colour.

Clean and stylish, just like the passing that characterised the Spurs team that wore it, the shirt graced the glorious Double-winning season having been introduced in 1959/60, Nicholson's first full campaign as the club's manager.

Having secured the league title in mid-April 1961, the campaign culminated in the FA Cup final against Leicester City, which prompted the production of a bespoke set of shirts with the match detail 'WEMBLEY 1961' boldly embroidered beneath the crest.

Unusually, Spurs failed to dazzle at Wembley but still ran out 2-0 winners to secure the FA Cup and become the first side in the 20th century to achieve the Double, something many had regarded as an impossible feat.

The shirt featured here was worn by full-back Peter Baker, one of the unsung heroes among the star-studded Lilywhites, whose reliability, composure, athleticism and innate understanding of the game played a significant part in providing the foundation for all the magic that took place further up the field.

*The Spurs players, including Peter Baker (second from left), proudly parade the FA Cup trophy at Wembley after completing the historic league and cup Double*

# FA CUP FINAL 1961

*Match worn shirt and tracksuit of* DANNY BLANCHFLOWER

This tracksuit jacket belonging to legendary captain Danny Blanchflower was one of two in different styles issued to the players before the final. This was the warm-up jacket and not the 'walkout' top worn when he led the team out of the Wembley tunnel

*On the shirt itself the black cloth stitch-applied number has faded over time but this does nothing to diminish its place in the history of Tottenham Hotspur Football Club*

# FA CUP FINAL 1962

*Match worn by* MAURICE NORMAN

Exactly 364 days after beating Leicester City to secure the Double, Spurs were back at Wembley in an attempt to retain the most famous club trophy in the world.

Bill Nicholson's men ran out once again in the same short-sleeved v-neck lilywhite shirts that had graced their Double season, the only obvious change from the previous year's showpiece being the match detail. The year '1962' and the word 'WEMBLEY' were embroidered beneath the shield-encased club crest.

The numbers on the backs of the shirts were again made from black cloth in the usual Umbro font and were stitched on to the jerseys.

With two teams committed to attacking, progressive football the final itself was an entertaining match, but in the end Spurs proved too much for Burnley and ran out comfortable 3-1 winners thanks to goals from Jimmy Greaves and Bobby Smith in addition to a Danny Blanchflower penalty. Centre-half Maurice Norman, who wore the shirt pictured here, was the defensive heartbeat of the side.

Match worn shirts from such occasions are extremely rare and very special. Similar-looking shirts do surface from time to time online or at auction, but many of these are 'replicas' which would have been supplied to sports shops by Umbro marketing reps for use in window displays during the build-up to a big game like a cup final. These shirts always differed from the player jerseys, with the crest and detail usually embroidered on to a woolen patch and then stitched to the jersey, unlike the player shirts where the crest was embroidered directly on to the shirt.

*Above: John White and Maurice Norman (right) hold the FA Cup trophy aloft following Spurs' 3-1 victory over Burnley*

*Above: Umbro's 'Choice of Champions' tag was entirely appropriate on the shirt labels of the 1961 and 1962 double FA Cup winners*

# CUP WINNERS' CUP FINAL 1963

*Match worn by* DANNY BLANCHFLOWER

By now short-sleeved jerseys with v-necks were giving way to long-sleeved, crew-necked shirts, and Spurs followed fashion for the start of their European Cup Winners' Cup campaign in October 1962.

Unveiled for the first round first leg game away to Glasgow Rangers, the new shirts were made from Umbro's shrink-resistant Tangeru cotton. The template style was actually listed in the manufacturer's catalogue as 'Real Jersey' and this may have contributed to the myth that Spurs wore all-white in Europe in honour of the legendary Real Madrid team of the time, whereas in fact the decision to go with an all-white colour combination for matches played under floodlights goes back to the mid 1950s.

When Tottenham ran out at Ibrox the shirt was distinctively 'Spurs', with a thin cloth patch containing the printed (rather than embroidered) navy cockerel in a shield crest stitched to the jersey. Unlike the two previous cup final appearances, for the subsequent final in Rotterdam there was no bespoke match detail embroidery added to the set of standard league shirts used.

Originating from the personal collection of Danny Blanchflower, it is impossible to over-emphasise the rarity of the shirt pictured here, the lack of distinguishing match detail meaning that even in the extremely unlikely event that any other examples have survived they would be virtually impossible to attribute to this game without cast-iron provenance.

Spurs had agonisingly just failed to reach the European Cup final the previous season, but after winning the FA Cup in 1962 they earned a second crack at continental glory with entry into the European Cup Winners' Cup and they reached the final where they faced holders Atletico Madrid.

In the match, Spurs let their football do the talking with a breathtaking display to defeat Atletico 5-1 and – led by their iconic skipper – become the first British team to win a major European trophy.

*Above: Spurs skipper Danny Blanchflower shakes hands with his Atletico Madrid counterpart before the 1963 Cup Winners' Cup final*

*Right: The numbers of the period tended to fade over time. Fortunately Blanchflower's signature, within the shield of the club crest, has survived*

# BRILLIANT WHITES

Tottenham fans are often mocked for dwelling on the past – but when that history is so rich, is it any wonder the memories of what became known as the 'glory glory years' have barely subsided more than 50 years on?

Under the guidance of legendary manager Bill Nicholson, the colours of lilywhite and blue became synonymous not just with success but with success achieved in the right way – in style. During the glorious 1960/61 season Spurs set record after record on their way to an era-defining league and cup Double, earning the mantle 'Super Spurs'. But they weren't stopping there. Nicholson, ever the ambitious purist, now set his sights on taking on the best that Europe had to offer.

What sets great managers like Nicholson apart is the constant search to discover areas where even the slightest advantage might be gained. The great man would obsessively seek out small details which could make a difference to player performance, and that included the playing kit. 'Bill Nick' was a pioneer of the school of thought that considered style in terms of a potential performance advantage – the 'if you look smart you play smart' ethos. This was of course an era when the team manager had influence over all aspects of the football club, and that included having the final say on the club's kit colour and design.

This attention to detail in terms of the playing strip was seen in Bill Nick's first full season in charge of Spurs, when he changed the home shirt to Umbro's lighter cotton, short-sleeved v-neck 'Continental' (later 'International') style. And there was a further twist to the club's home strip for Tottenham's debut on the European stage.

When the team ran out for their first-ever competitive European fixture against Polish side Gornik Zabrze in September 1961, the players were wearing white shorts

## "I ABSOLUTELY LOVED PLAYING IN ALL-WHITE, IT MADE YOU FEEL 10 FEET TALL, UNBEATABLE"
### PHIL BEAL

rather than their traditional navy. The match represents the very beginning of the club's glorious European history and the start of a unique tradition whereby Spurs – other than for a handful of exceptions during the 1990s – have always worn white shorts with their white shirts and socks when playing in continental competition.

The popular story is that the team adopted this all-white strip for its pioneering ventures into continental football because of Bill Nicholson's admiration for the all-conquering Real Madrid side of the late 1950s. But did Bill Nick – like one of his playing and managerial peers of the period, Don Revie, who insisted during the summer of 1961 that Leeds United permanently adopt an all-white kit in the style of Real Madrid – want his Spurs side to emulate the Spaniards, not just in how they played but how they looked? The truth of the matter – like the fact that Spurs did not copy Preston North End when switching their colours to white and navy – is almost certainly less romantic but sheds further light on the genius of Bill Nicholson and his meticulous attention to every detail.

Spurs had actually been experimenting with the team strip for some time, especially as a means of improving player visibility in floodlit games. These were the early days of floodlights (the first league match under lights was not played until 1956) and the lights themselves were of a much lesser quality than those we are familiar with today, meaning playing conditions could be gloomy to say the least. So one of Nicholson's innovations when he took over as manager in 1958 was to introduce an alternative change kit to the club's traditional (and Nicholson's favoured) dark navy shirts, bringing in an alternative change strip of all-amber which he thought would help the players to see each other more clearly under lights.

Going back even further to September 1956 – when Nicholson was assistant to Jimmy Anderson – Spurs

wore white shorts as part of a home strip for the first time in a floodlit friendly against Racing Club de Paris. Indeed, not only did they play the match in all-white, they also experimented with shirts made from a shiny, reflective material known as Rayon. The idea was that the combination of all-white and the shiny material would help the players to see each other in the murky light. Two weeks later the same kit got a run-out for the Anglo-Scottish Floodlit League home game with Partick Thistle; the programme for that match describing Spurs as playing in 'Corinthian all-white'.

*Above: This picture from Spurs' first-ever home European Cup match in 1961 illustrates the practical thinking behind the decision to wear white shorts*

*Previous pages: The 1963 European Cup Winners' Cup winners are resplendent in their all-white strip*

The Rayon shirts were ditched after a handful of games because the material was very hot and uncomfortable for the players (although an amber change kit made from the same material was trialled in 1958), but the idea of white shorts for improved visibility in floodlit games prevailed. Under Bill Nicholson's management, an all-white kit was worn away to Wolverhampton Wanderers in March 1959, with white shirts and shorts worn – albeit with blue socks – away to Sheffield Wednesday during the 1959/60 season, as well as for a floodlit friendly match against Torpedo Moscow in November 1959, when the fact that the game was played in fog almost certainly reinforced the logic behind the idea.

So although Nicholson, like many in football, admired Real Madrid, the extraordinary winners of the first five European Cups, the reason for the decision to wear white shorts for European matches – always played in midweek and usually under floodlights – was far less romantic. It was a purely practical choice aimed at maximising player performance. The fact that Real Madrid also played in all-white is a coincidence, although the myth may well have been perpetuated by the fact that when they became the first British winners of a European trophy by winning the European Cup Winners' Cup in 1963 the Spurs players were not just wearing the same colours as the famous Spanish team but the exact same style of Umbro jersey. The shirt that many consider the classic Spurs shirt even appeared in the Umbro catalogue as the 'Real' jersey and was, according to the manufacturer, "the choice of the world famous team Real Madrid, and many other leading British teams".

Ironically, the game away to Gornik in Poland – the first occasion when Spurs wore white shorts designed to improve visibility in a competitive European match – was played in daylight. However, Nicholson had made his decision and the tradition had begun, although this appears to have been lost on the Spurs stars who played in the match.

"We just turned up in the dressing room for the game and there was the all-white kit," Cliff Jones recalls. "No-one said anything; nothing was said to us. We just focused on the game coming up."

"Nobody ever mentioned Real Madrid, ever," concurs Phil Beal. "Although I absolutely loved playing in all-white, it made you feel 10 feet tall, unbeatable." And Ricky George, a young apprentice at the time, concurs: "The all-white kit was for visibility. It was Bill Nick's way of looking for those marginal gains. Those nights at White Hart Lane, under the lights, were just very special."

"We loved playing in all-white," continues Jones. "I honestly cannot say for certain it made any difference in making us see each other better under the floodlights, but we did love playing in it. European nights we felt fresher, the air was different."

The late, great, Alan Gilzean put it slightly more succinctly. "It just felt special," he said.

*Above, left: A page from the Umbro catalogue advertising the 'Real' style of jersey – worn by both Spurs and Real Madrid – which is one of the sources of the myth that Bill Nicholson chose all-white for Europe in homage to the great Spanish team*

*Above: This club crest, which has been cut off a shirt, is the only surviving evidence of the experimental 'gold' change kit introduced by Bill Nicholson to improve player visibility in floodlit games*

*Left: Danny Blanchflower with the European Cup Winners' Cup trophy after Spurs became the first British team to win a European trophy by beating Atletico Madrid in 1963*

*The cover of the Umbro teamwear catalogue for the 1961/62 season featured the famous picture of the 1961 champions*

# THE CHOICE OF CHAMPIONS

Spurs might have been the Double-winners, the team of the moment and famous the world over, but during the glorious heyday of the early 1960s the club's kit operation was remarkably primitive. At this time even major football clubs did not have big money kit deals with manufacturers like they do today; instead they selected what style they wanted to play in from the catalogue of their chosen manufacturer (essentially Umbro or Bukta) and then ordered it through a local sports retailer.

Since the 1950s Tottenham Hotspur had used Geo. Elsey & Son, a sports shop on the Tottenham High Road that also had branches in Chiswick and Palmers Green, to order their preferred Umbro kit. Every season around six complete new sets of home kit were ordered, with Bill Nicholson selecting the lighter 'International Soccer Jersey' from the Umbro range in 'Self Style' which meant the collars and cuffs were the same colour as the main body of the shirt, i.e. white. Elseys would place the order with Umbro, including all the details such as the club crest and the colour and style of the numbers.

After the Double was achieved, Umbro were keen to let the world know that it had been achieved in their kit. The success spawned numerous advertisements and the famous picture of the Spurs team at White Hart Lane featured on the cover of its 1961/62 catalogue (left and above right). The 'Umbrochure' also featured an introduction from Manchester United manager Matt Busby, which demonstrates how forward-thinking football bosses like Busby and Bill Nick were beginning to understand the importance of player comfort to performance.

An insight into the way the kit operation worked in these days can be gleaned from a letter (right) from Bill Nicholson to the club's representative at Umbro, Jim Terris, thanking the manufacturer for the excellent service in securing two extra large shirts, believed to be for giant centre-half Maurice Norman, at late notice. The Mr Boyle referred to in the letter was the club's contact at Geo. Elsey & Son.

Umbro were also the sole UK distributor for adidas boots (far right), which the Spurs players all wore, and again the team's Double success allowed them to market the fact they were the suppliers of both playing kit and footwear to their flagship club.

# HOME 1963-66

*Match worn by* JIMMY GREAVES

From 1963 to 1966 Spurs wore their now standard crew-necked 'Real Jersey' template shirts in keeping with the fashion of the time, and although these shirts were only available from manufacturers Umbro in long sleeves, on occasion some Spurs players would appear in short-sleeved versions. These short-sleeved shirts were not manufactured as such, but were long-sleeved shirts individually tailored for player comfort on the express instruction of Bill Nicholson.

Nicholson – the master of finding any area of the club or the team where he could make small changes to try to improve performance – had noticed that some of his players were often rolling up their sleeves. Long before the importance of match kit design was even considered by most managers, the forward-thinking Spurs boss realised that there could be a benefit in offering his players the option of a short-sleeved jersey. The theory was simple: 'If they feel good, they will play better'.

To achieve the desired effect, Nicholson ordered that standard long-sleeved shirts be sent to a local seamstress, who would cut down the sleeves then remove the cuffs and reapply them where the sleeves now ended.

With these shirts generally only used on tours to hot countries or on warm days, shirts like this No.8, worn by the great Jimmy Greaves, are extremely rare. Apart from the fact that very few were produced, the club's coach and kit room guardian, Johnny Wallis, strictly enforced his rule of not allowing players to keep any shirts. Once they were deemed not pristine enough for the first team, they would be handed down to the reserves, the A team, and after that – if they still survived – they would be used as training kit for the youth team. Eventually they would be cut into rags and used by the apprentices for cleaning duties. The letter 'A' which appears at the bottom of this shirt is a marking from Wallis' famous kit labelling system, and indicates that it had been handed down to the A team and was therefore almost certainly signed by Greaves some years later.

*Above: This shirt has an older style 'Choice of Champions' Umbro logo*

*Left: Jimmy Greaves in action in the long-sleeved version of this jersey. There are no known photographs of the short-sleeved tailored shirts in action*

*Right: The screen-printed club crest that appeared on these shirts was slightly different from the previous fully embroidered woollen version*

# HOME 1963–65

*Match worn by* RON HENRY

Between 1963 and 1965, there were some variations to the regular Umbro home jersey, as seen on this wonderful, rare and signed Ron Henry shirt which features the printed club crest but this time unusually placed on a square cloth patch. It is not known why, at this time, some examples of the crest were produced this way, rather than embroidered on to cloth which was then cut around the shield before being sewn on to the jersey. It was definitely a cheaper method of production, although it did result in a slightly faded, lighter crest after a few washes.

These square printed patches also appeared on some of the rarest Spurs shirts of this period, those produced not by Umbro but by rival supplier Bukta and known to have been first used during the 1964/65 season.

At various times during the 1960s the players' training kit was made by Bukta and we now know that at least one set of match shirts was acquired and worn on occasion by at least some members of the first team – although few examples have survived. Photographic evidence tells us that Bukta shirts were used in the 1964/65 pre-season photocall, although it is not known how many matches the shirts were actually used for and by how many players.

During this period, the crest on the shirt was also evolving, and on the opening day of the 1965 season the first-ever incarnation of the now iconic club crest – featuring a cockerel standing on a ball without the surrounding shield – appeared on at least some of the players' shirts for the match against Leicester City in August 1965, and again v Liverpool the following month.

Inspired by the gold cockerel-and-ball statue which by now had been roosting at White Hart Lane for 46 years, this new version of the crest disappeared from the Spurs shirt for the rest of the season as the club reverted to the old shield-encased design before re-appearing – in a number of subtly different incarnations – as the crest of choice on the club's shirts from the start of the 1966/67 season.

*Above: Cliff Jones celebrates scoring in a Bukta shirt from the early 1960s, when Umbro shirts were also worn*

*Above: A rare Bukta Spurs shirt that also has the club crest on a square patch, as well as a pristine manufacturer's collar label*

# HOME 1966/67

*Match worn by* JOE KINNEAR

This extremely rare match worn shirt from the 1966/67 season is distinctive because of its unusual embroidered club crest. This is actually the second incarnation of the now famous Spurs crest design featuring the cockerel on a ball without the surrounding shield, but unusually the vintage-style ball upon which this navy cockerel is standing is brown.

This particular shirt can be dated to this particular season because of the Umbro collar label which celebrates England's 1966 World Cup win. There is no photographic evidence of this style of badge ever being worn in a match, although it does appear on Pat Jennings' shirt on a cigarette card produced at the time. If it was worn it is likely to have been during the first month of the season as a revised version of the crest incorporating a blue ball appeared in September.

A key milestone in the evolution of the club crest, not only is the ball upon which the cockerel stands brown, the panels on it are now diagonally aligned as opposed to front-on, which is how they appeared on the crest's first incarnation (used for three games the previous season).

Like all Umbro player shirts at this time, this example was made from the manufacturer's trademark Tangeru cotton. We know this particular jersey is genuine as it originated from Joe Kinnear's personal memorabilia collection, later being sold at auction. Irishman Kinnear was a skilful full-back in the finest Spurs tradition and represented the new breed of Tottenham player in Bill Nicholson's second great side.

*Left: Joe Kinnear in action against Arsenal in September 1967, the season after the unusual club crest with a blue cockerel on a brown ball made an appearance*

*Below: Pat Jennings appears on a football sticker with his goalkeeper's shirt adorned with the little-known brown ball crest (left)*

*Above: The shirt's Umbro collar label celebrates England's 1966 World Cup win and dates it to the 1966/67 season*

# HOME 1966/67

*Match worn by* FRANK SAUL

During the 1966/67 season Spurs took to the field for at least three matches wearing shirts not made by their usual kit manufacturer, Umbro, but by rival supplier Bukta. These shirts carried the third incarnation of the shieldless cockerel-and-ball crest – with the ball returning to blue – which would remain unchanged for many years and become the club's iconic badge now recognised the world over.

Widely considered the oldest football kit manufacturer, Stockport-based Bukta were founded in 1879. For almost a century Bukta and Umbro were the two dominant football kit brands, much like Nike and adidas are today, and by the 1960s Bukta had supplied around 50 Football League clubs as well as – between 1960 and 1965 – the England team.

Exactly why Spurs wore Bukta shirts – at this time more traditionally used as the club's training kit – for these matches is not known. Photographs from the season suggests that Bukta shirts were worn in three games, including the one pictured against Liverpool on 1 April 1967 when this No.11 shirt was worn by Frank Saul. The shirt was donned by Welsh wing wizard Cliff Jones in the other two games in which it was worn.

The new crest was printed on to a rectangular cloth patch, with the ball in a more familiar navy blue as opposed to the brown that appeared on some of the shirts of the time. Later Umbro shirts featuring the new design had the crest embroidered directly on to the shirt, which is how we are able to distinguish between the two manufacturers when studying match photographs. The font used for the numbers also differed between the manufacturers, which helps with identification.

The 'A11' marked at the bottom of shirt's front is part of Johnny Wallis' unique code and indicates that once deemed no longer suitable for the first team it became part of a second set for the A team. The damage seen on the collar label is evidence that it would likely later have been used as training kit.

Above: Spurs trio Jimmy Robertson (left), goalscorer Jimmy Greaves (centre) and Dave Mackay celebrate scoring against Liverpool in April 1967, one of three games Bukta shirts are known to have been worn in

Above: A Bukta label is stitched into the hem as well as the collar of this unusual shirt. The numbers on the Bukta Spurs home shirts of this time were smaller than on their Umbro equivalents (right)

# FA CUP FINAL 1967

*Match worn by* ALAN GILZEAN

The 1966/67 season saw something of a Spurs revival with the team finishing third in the league, just four points behind champions Manchester United, but the undoubted highlight came when Tottenham reached another FA Cup final at Wembley.

In the run-up to the first-ever all-London FA Cup final, Chelsea won the toss to see which of the two clubs would be the designated 'home' team and chose to wear their traditional blue, which meant Spurs would wear all-white. The FA, however, instructed Chelsea to wear blue socks instead of their normal white and Spurs to wear white shorts instead of their usual navy "in order to provide a contrast with opposing colours".

Spurs told supporters that despite the slight departure from their first-choice kit they would be keeping up with club tradition "by including a touch of blue in our Wembley strip". This took the form of the club crest, the Umbro font cloth stitched numbers and an unusual navy stripe down each side of the players' shorts.

Tottenham's match shirts for the final had a special 'Wembley 1967' match detail scroll also in navy embroidered beneath the new cockerel-and-ball crest and the team marked the occasion with a dominant performance not reflected in the narrow 2-1 scoreline.

The shirt pictured was worn in the final by the original 'King of White Hart Lane', Alan Gilzean, and later sold at auction. However, as was the custom at the time, more than one set of shirts for the cup final were provided by Umbro, and in era when kit men by necessity would make the maximum use of all available kit, some of these shirts – complete with the 'Wembley 1967' scroll – went on to be worn in three consecutive matches at the start of the following season; a win over Sunderland, a home draw with Sheffield United, and a win at Coventry. And the shorts with the navy trim worn at Wembley were also used for the following season's European Cup Winners' Cup campaign.

*Above: Alan Gilzean (right), Mike England (centre) and Frank Saul (left) celebrate winning the 1967 FA Cup. It was not unusual for Spurs to wear white shorts. In fact the combination of white shirts and shorts was worn in every FA Cup game that season except for the fourth round against Portsmouth and the semi-final against Nottingham Forest*

*Above: The Umbro collar label from Gilzean's 'medium' size shirt*

# HOME 1967/68

*Match worn by* CLIFF JONES

With the now familiar navy cockerel-and-ball crest neatly embroidered directly into the shirt, this is an early example of the classic Umbro long-sleeved Aztec-style, crew-necked Spurs shirt of the late 1960s and early 1970s which is fondly remembered for its clean, pure lilywhite simplicity.

The two dots at the bottom of the front of this shirt would have been marked by kit man Johnny Wallis. The dots here signify that this belonged to the second set of shirts worn by the senior team during this season – there being a maximum of four sets normally used per campaign.

Manufactured from Umbro's much-improved shrink-resistant Tangeru cotton, this No.11 shirt was worn by Cliff Jones during his last full season at Spurs. It came from Jones' personal collection and was sold at auction.

Long before the arrival of Gareth Bale, Jones was the original 'Welsh Wizard' on the wing for Spurs. He scored 159 goals from 372 appearances for the Lilywhites – a phenomenal strike rate for a winger. Just six years on from the epic Double, Bill Nicholson was still in charge, assembling another side to pursue and win trophies. This season was to prove Jones' effective swansong, as the last of the legends of '61 left at the club departed Tottenham for Fulham in October 1968.

*Above: Cliff Jones puts West Ham goalkeeper Bobby Ferguson under pressure in August 1967*

*Right: The No.11 on the back of this shirt is in the Umbro font, the digits being in navy and slightly longer than seen on the previous season's Bukta shirt*

# LEAGUE CUP FINAL 1971

*Match worn by* ALAN MULLERY

As the 1970s began, Bill Nicholson's rebuilt Spurs side reached the League Cup final and, apart from delivering the club's first trophy for four years, the match is remembered for the unusual strip that Spurs wore.

At the time, Football League rules stipulated that if any component (shirt, shorts or socks) of the two teams' kit clashed in the League Cup competition, each team had to change. As both Tottenham Hotspur and Aston Villa's first-choice socks were white both finalists were required to make changes, with Spurs electing to wear their yellow away socks.

All this was straightforward enough, but more unusually Spurs then took the decision to wear the royal blue shorts of the forthcoming season's away kit, rather than the club's traditional navy. And even more controversially to some, for the set of shirts manufactured for the final the club crest, match detail embroidery and numbers were all produced in the same royal blue as the shorts. Even the tracksuits for the final featured this lighter and untraditional shade of blue on the trim and the word 'SPURS' on the back. Beneath the crest, the text 'FL CUP' (the FL standing for 'Football League') and 'WEMBLEY 1971' appeared over two lines.

This one-off shirt featured a subtle Umbro stamp positioned to the bottom right of the front of the shirt – just above the hem – in royal blue. This was a regular feature of the club's shirts from 1966 onwards, although it faded quickly and eventually disappeared when laundered, and this shirt, having been worn only once, is the first known example on which it has survived.

The League Cup had grown in stature since its initial introduction when it was regarded as an inconvenience for the top clubs. The decision to award the winners a place in European football via the new UEFA Cup – a revamped version of the Inter-Cities Fairs Cup – swayed the doubters. And so it was that Spurs were reacquainted with continental opposition thanks to their 2-0 triumph.

*Above: Spurs captain Alan Mullery shakes hands with Aston Villa's Brian Godfrey before the final*

*Right: Umbro, now using 'Umbro International' on its collar labels, produced cup final jerseys that featured the company's branding on the outside in the form of a stamp*

# HOME 1971–75, UEFA CUP FINAL 1972

*Match worn by* RALPH COATES

With the club crest and numbers restored to navy following the brief flirtation with royal blue for the 1971 League Cup final, this classically stylish jersey is considered by many to be *the* Spurs shirt.

Going virtually unchanged over the course of the next six seasons, the iconic Umbro Aztec 'Self Colour Association' style in pure unadulterated lilywhite, save for the proud navy crest, has come to symbolise Tottenham in the Seventies – a seminal shirt for the age and a touchstone design for future nostalgia.

Worn during a period when the club increasingly struggled to make an impact at the top end of the First Division table, this style of jersey nevertheless was worn in two UEFA Cup finals – both legs of the victory over Wolverhampton Wanderers in 1972, and in the drawn first leg of the eventual defeat to Feyenoord two years later. On both occasions the shirts worn in the final were unembellished with any match detail embroidery.

Martin Chivers remembers asking Johnny Wallis if he could keep his shirt after he scored twice in the first leg of the 1972 final. "But he said 'No, you'll need it for the second leg'. After the second leg I asked him if I could have it and he said 'No, I need it for the reserves next season!'"

The No.11 shirt featured here can be dated to the early 1970s by the collar label and does not include the Umbro stamp, which has almost certainly been completely washed out, and Wallis' coding system of dots and letters can be found inside the front of the hem as opposed to on the outside where he had previously placed them.

Whilst still in use by the first team, the jersey would have been worn primarily by Ralph Coates, one of Bill Nicholson's last-ever signings who arrived from Burnley in 1971 and became a hugely popular figure among teammates and fans alike. Other less regular incumbents of the No.11 shirt during this era were Alan Gilzean, Jimmy Pearce and Jimmy Neighbour.

*Mike England, Alan Gilzean, Ralph Coates and Joe Kinnear, with Martin Chivers standing behind, pose with the UEFA Cup in 1972*

# LEAGUE CUP FINAL 1973

*Match shirt of* MARTIN PETERS

For Tottenham's second Football League Cup final appearance in three years, the club returned to their traditional navy crest (with accompanying match embroidery) after the brief departure into royal blue for the 1971 occasion.

The classic long-sleeved shirts from the era were complemented with the words 'FL CUP' (no mention of the final) and 'WEMBLEY 1973' over two lines beneath the cockerel-and-ball crest, with the usual stitch-applied navy Umbro numbers on the back.

This was the very beginning of the era when manufacturers' branding started to appear on club shirts, but while both Leeds and Sunderland would sport Umbro's double diamond logo on their shirts for the FA Cup final two months later, there was no such adornment on Spurs' lilywhite jerseys at Wembley. However, the logo did appear on Pat Jennings' blue goalkeeper's shirt – worn rather than the traditional green – as well as, for the first time, on the white shorts worn by all the Spurs players.

Spurs wore white shorts for the final because of the demands of television, with the broadcasters deeming the change necessary to provide enough of a distinction between the two teams (Norwich wore their traditional yellow shirts and green shorts), especially for those watching in black and white.

Spurs' second League Cup triumph in three years came after a frustrating final. Only when Ralph Coates struck in the 72nd minute could Spurs break Norwich City's suffocating tactics. Their opponents had opted for a massed defence and this stifled the Lilywhites' attacking intent, in particular by nullifying skipper Martin Peters.

*Let the celebrations begin! In an era where long-sleeved shirts were the norm, Steve Perryman's rolled-up sleeves give a glimpse into the future of kit style. Goalkeeper Pat Jennings can be seen in his unusual blue jersey (also right), complete with the Umbro logo*

# AWAY 1971–75, UEFA CUP FINAL 1974

*Match worn by* TERRY NAYLOR

For the majority of the 1960s, navy was Tottenham Hotspur's first-choice change shirt colour. Initially the shirts had a white v-neck and cuffs, and from the 1962/63 season onwards the design changed to a white crew-neck and cuffs. No examples of these much-loved jerseys have survived, although they have subsequently become extremely popular retro replica shirts.

However, with television beginning to play a much bigger role in the coverage of the game, in 1969 the Football League banned teams from wearing navy shirts because – on black and white TVs especially – they were confusingly similar to the black traditionally worn by match officials. In 1969, therefore, Spurs introduced their first yellow away jersey following advice from distributor Ron Goodman that it was a vibrant colour that clashed with the fewest number of other teams' home strips.

Tottenham wore yellow for the first time for the opening game of the 1969/70 season away to Leeds United. Like their navy predecessors, these jerseys featured white trim and also white numbers which proved extremely hard to read. The style was only worn for two seasons and no examples are known to have survived.

For the 1971/72 season, the white trim was dropped and the club switched to the all-yellow Umbro Aztec 'Self Colour Association' style with a navy embroidered club crest as pictured here, essentially a yellow reverse version of the classic white home shirt. The new style received its first airing away to Leeds on the opening day of the season and was worn – with royal blue shorts and numbers – for the following four campaigns.

The shirt pictured here – the earliest example of a yellow Spurs jersey in this collection – was worn by Terry Naylor for the ill-fated second leg of the 1974 UEFA Cup final. The jersey, which does not feature any bespoke cup final embroidery, was swapped after the match with a Feyenoord player and only resurfaced during the course of researching this book.

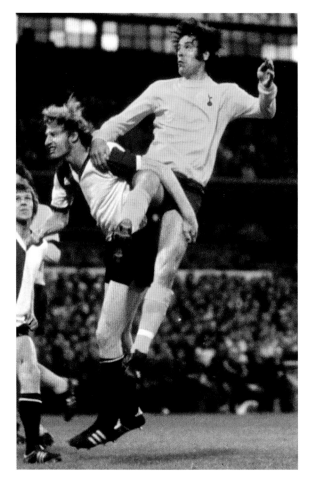

*Left: The 1974 UEFA Cup final second leg was a disastrous one for Spurs. Not only did they lose 2-0 in Rotterdam (having drawn 2-2 in the first leg at White Hart Lane) but the occasion was marred by hooliganism. The events off the pitch, with some Spurs fans rioting during the match, shocked Bill Nicholson profoundly and the night marked the beginning of the end of his glory glory era. Centre-half Mike England is pictured in action during the infamous match*

# HOME 1974/75

*Match shirt of* JIMMY NEIGHBOUR

During the 1970s, short-sleeved shirts began to come back into fashion in English football. The trend stemmed from Umbro's creation of a special 'Airtex' shirt for the England team (and others including West Germany) for the 1970 World Cup that was played in the searing heat of Mexico. Forward-thinking as ever, Bill Nicholson ordered Airtex shirts in short sleeves for Spurs in 1972, but with the perforated fabric being much lighter than their full cotton counterparts these were only used in the early months of the 1972/73 and 1973/74 seasons and no known examples have survived.

The Airtex shirts still went against the general trend of the time which was for long-sleeved shirts, and indeed Umbro still didn't make Tottenham's favoured style of jersey in short sleeves. But, having noticed that some of his team – including Terry Naylor and Steve Perryman – would regularly roll their sleeves up in all weathers and at all times of year, Bill Nicholson decided that his players should have the option of short sleeves for every game.

It is important to remember that during the 1960s and 1970s clubs did not have kit deals with the manufacturers as they do today. They ordered their team kit through independent sports outfitters and therefore could only select from their chosen manufacturer's available range.

With short sleeves not available, Bill Nick – aware of the importance of player comfort to performance – returned to the idea of having a seamstress, this time an in-house member of the laundry room staff, individually tailor long-sleeved jerseys as required. As with the 1963 Jimmy Greaves example, the seamstress would cut down the arms of a standard home jersey, trim the cuffs off the unwanted sections and sew them back on to the new, shorter sleeves.

The No.14 shirt featured here, therefore, is an extremely rare example of such a shirt, which would have been worn or at least prepared for use sometime during the 1974/75 season, the first campaign when the Spurs team played in a mixture of long and short-sleeved shirts.

*Spurs, wearing Airtex shirts, take on Leeds United early in the 1973/74 season at White Hart Lane*

# HOME 1975–77

*Match shirt of* MARTIN CHIVERS

As well as being the first season when their classic shirt became available in bespoke short sleeves, the 1975/76 campaign saw a subtle but highly significant change to the famous lilywhite jersey – for the first time a manufacturer's logo was added to the right breast.

With the tradition of players having the choice of short or long sleeves now established, Spurs requested – via distributor Ron Goodman – that Umbro produce their traditional Aztec 'Association Self Coloured' shirts in short sleeves. Umbro agreed on the condition that, in an era of increasing commercialisation, Spurs allow their shirts to carry the company's double diamond logo.

The change happened virtually overnight, with the famous Umbro logo appearing on the short-sleeved shirts that were worn for the opening day home fixture against Middlesbrough, having been absent on the long-sleeved shirts worn in the pre-season team photograph.

Another significant change for the 1975/76 season was an increase in the size of the club crest, an alteration suggested by new manager Terry Neill. It was "to give the old crest a lift," he said. "We have a unique emblem, and should all be proud of the great traditions the cockerel represents – ours is more than just another white shirt."

The large cockerel crest was short-lived as things didn't work out at Spurs for Neill, who would go on to become boss of rivals Arsenal, and for the 1976/77 season – on the instruction of Neill's successor Keith Burkinshaw – Spurs reverted to the original, smaller club crest.

The shirt pictured was actually prepared, for Martin Chivers for the 1976/77 campaign, hence the small version of the crest. Because of his huge frame, Chivers required a longer cut of shirt than the norm (as did Mike England and Pat Jennings) and a twist in this tale is that any No.9 shirt ordered for him would automatically become part of a set of first team kit, meaning that when Chivers left the club in the summer of 1976 his replacement, Chris Jones, was saddled with an extra long shirt whether he liked it or not.

*The unmistakable Martin Chivers in action during the 1975/76 season, when the famous cockerel on a ball club crest was increased in size on the instructions of manager Terry Neill*

# AWAY 1975–77

*Match shirt of A SUBSTITUTE*

Whilst the white home shirt remained true to tradition despite the changing times, the introduction of a fashionable navy winged button-up collar on the yellow away shirt meant that – despite struggling on the pitch – Spurs were very much keeping up with current trends.

Yellow had become a very popular choice of away kit for many clubs in the 1970s, inspired in part by Brazil's sensational 1970 World Cup win. But Spurs had actually worn yellow the season before Pele and co. demolished Italy in the heat of Mexico.

For the start of the 1975/76 season, however, a new design ('Association Self Trim Button Collar') was chosen from the Umbro range which reintroduced an additional colour – other than the club crest – to the away jersey. The stylish collar and cuffs in traditional navy complemented the addition of the Umbro logo and the enhanced cockerel-and-ball crest that first appeared in 1975 on the suggestion of manager Terry Neill.

The result was a stylish and popular shirt that in some ways signalled the club's arrival in a new era of fashion-inspired football design.

Over the course of its two-season lifespan, this jersey saw plenty of action. It was used 12 times during the 1975/76 campaign and even more in its second season. And even though the cockerel reverted to its smaller version in 1976/77 (as was the case with the home shirt) there were occasions during the season when shirts with large and small crests were worn during the same game.

The shirt pictured is a very rare surviving example of the style. It has remained intact primarily because of its number – 16 – which would have meant (with only one substitute and therefore only numbers 1-12 required for league and cup games) it could only ever be used in friendlies, on tour or for a photocall where the back would not be visible.

*Ralph Coates on the ball in the long-sleeved version of this classic Spurs away jersey, which was the variation most commonly worn by the team*

# COME THE REVOLUTION
## 1977–1991

ADMIRAL, LE COQ SPORTIF & HUMMEL

# COME THE REVOLUTION

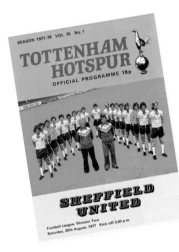

*Above: The new Admiral shirt made its league debut at home to Sheffield United on 20 August 1977*

*Far right: Argentinian World Cup stars Ossie Ardiles (left) and Ricky Villa (centre) – resplendent in the groundbreaking Spurs Admiral kit – are unveiled at the pre-season photocall before the 1978/79 campaign*

The mid 1970s heralded a whole new era for the Spurs shirt as the relationship between football clubs and their kit manufacturers moved from the boot room to the boardroom and the football kit market – along with the Tottenham Hotspur jersey – was changed forever.

During the Seventies the rulebook for football shirt design was torn up and thrown out of the window. Club shirts that had barely changed for decades were suddenly adorned with all manner of new colours, logos, stripes, details and trims. Up until now, football clubs had obtained their team kit not directly from the major manufacturers like Umbro and Bukta, but through a sportswear distributor. The market was dominated by small, local, family-owned independent sports shops like Goodman Sports in Southgate, who had been supplying Umbro playing kit to Tottenham Hotspur since the mid-1960s. Spurs would place an order with Ron Goodman, who would order it from Umbro, usually at a discount – yes, the clubs paid for all their kit in these days – and Goodmans would supply the club.

At this time football managers had the overall say on everything to do with the football side of their club, and that included making the decisions on the kit. "The directors just left everything to me," remembers Keith Burkinshaw, Spurs manager between 1976 and 1984, who immediately after taking over ordered that the cockerel crest on the shirt revert back to its former size after his predecessor, Terry Neil, had increased it. "It was my decision. I spoke to the suppliers and manufacturers and we decided that's how the cockerel should be."

Whilst Spurs continued to operate in this way through the 1970s, away from north London the football kit landscape was changing rapidly. Although Umbrosets For Boys – full Umbro kits in generic colours which were sold in a box – had been around since 1959, by the early 1970s there was still no replica shirt market to speak of. Clubs sold far more scarves than shirts through their small club shops. Then along came Admiral.

Admiral was the brainchild of Bert Patrick. Patrick's revolutionary vision was the idea that rather than clubs paying manufacturers to purchase their kit, the manufacturer should pay the club to wear their strips in return for the right to not only brand the kit with its logos but, crucially, sell replicas aimed at the children's market.

Based in Leicester, Admiral's big break was a deal stuck with Don Revie's Leeds United to supply the kit for the 1973/74 league champions. And by the mid 1970s Admiral had signed deals with the likes of Manchester United, Luton Town and Coventry City, with the kits introducing vibrant new colours, racy stripes and multiple Admiral logos on to team shirts that had barely changed since the 1950s.

In 1974, Admiral signed a deal to supply the England national team, now managed by a certain Don Revie. This was Patrick's big moment, the FA agreeing a contract that would earn them £15,000 per year or a 10 per cent royalty on shirt sales, whichever was the greater, with the Admiral England shirts not only featuring the manufacturer's logo but broad red and blue stripes down the arms. The design was not popular with the the traditionalists, but the kids loved it. Indeed, for school-age boys into football an Admiral kit – even if it was not their country or team (the Wales kit featuring yellow and green tramlines down the front, for instance, was hugely popular all over England) – was the 'must-have' garment of the mid-1970s.

By the summer of 1977, after 27 seasons in the top flight, Tottenham Hotspur were relegated to Division Two and

## KIT DEALS MOVED FROM THE BOOTROOM TO THE BOARD-ROOM AND THE SPURS SHIRT WAS CHANGED FOREVER

*Above: A page from the 1978/79 Admiral catalogue showing some of the innovative club kit designs that the Leicester-based company had introduced*

*Above right: An extremely rare prototype Spurs Admiral away shirt. In the end the style featuring two navy 'half braces' was chosen and this style was never worn*

Patrick spied an opportunity. With the Spurs board sticking by their manager, he made contact with Keith Burkinshaw.

"We were aware that Ron Goodman had a great relationship with Tottenham Hotspur and offered a great service," explains Patrick. "But we were supplying clubs direct with kit, and paying royalties on replica sales, which we knew Goodmans couldn't offer."

Burkinshaw was highly aware that relegation would have an impact on the club's finances so jumped at the chance to discuss bringing Admiral on board. "He accepted our proposals and negotiated the whole deal himself," Patrick recalls.

And so, in the summer of 1977, Tottenham Hotspur Football Club signed its first-ever kit deal and, at a stroke, more than 40 years of wearing Umbro – aside from and a fleeting hiatus with Bukta – was ended. Admiral was shaking up the football industry with its designs and for the 1977/78 season the Spurs shirt underwent dramatic change. For the first time ever, navy trim appeared on a Spurs shirt. But it wasn't just a navy trim, both the collar and the stripe down the arms contained multiple Admiral logos within them.

Initially greeted with horror by those for whom pure and unadorned lilywhite was sacrosanct, a successful promotion season and then the arrival of Argentinian World Cup stars Ossie Ardiles and Ricky Villa helped assimilate the style into the supporters' affections and nowadays of course the shirt – and its corresponding tracksuit top – are considered retro classics. Best of all for the club, they were selling kits and making money.

"We knew that because of Spurs' history and strong support there was huge potential for replica shirt sales,"

## THE ADMIRAL SPURS KIT WAS GREETED WITH HORROR BY THOSE FOR WHOM PURE UNADORNED LILYWHITE WAS SACROSANCT

continues Patrick. "And when the two Argentinian players signed, we were able to use them a lot in our marketing, which increased our overseas sales of Spurs shirts."

Admiral signed a new contract with Spurs in April 1980, but by the summer the receivers had been called in at the company's Leicester HQ. They had hugely overstretched themselves and, according to Patrick's right-hand man, John Griffin, "borrowed too much money". Having revolutionised the design of football kit and the way it was supplied forever, despite having more than £1 million worth of orders on the books, the company went under (although the brand was sold on and the new company continued to supply England and a handful of clubs). The Admiral partnership with Spurs had lasted just three years, but a new manufacturer name was about to burst onto the UK football kit scene.

In the 1970s the German company adidas took legal action against Le Coq Sportif in France over the French company's production of designs featuring three stripes – the famous adidas trademark. Le Coq Sportif

and adidas had a licensing agreement, similar to its deal with Umbro in the UK that one company would market kit and the other footwear. So when adidas decided to move into sportswear it created a conflict. When the French court ruled against the German company's challenge over the use of the three stripes it angered the son of the company's founder Adi Dassler, Horst Dassler – who was running adidas's French operation and already owned shares in Le Coq Sportif – so much that he upped his stake in the French brand to 49 per cent.

Dassler junior was making a habit of buying into and taking over rival sports brands. He did the same with Pony, for instance. The rest of the Dassler family knew nothing about it. Then when – soon after the French court case – Le Coq Sportif ran into financial trouble, Horst's friend, Andre Guelfi, bailed them out which allowed the young Dassler to acquire the two per cent he needed to take a controlling interest in the company.

Then in 1977, and again with his parents back at adidas HQ in Germany completely unaware that he was systematically and surreptitiously attempting to buy up

*Left: A young Glenn Hoddle poses in the classic Admiral tracksuit which is remembered almost as fondly as the home shirt*

*Above: Ossie Ardiles in action against Crystal Palace in the yellow and navy Admiral away kit*

## "THE PLAYERS LOVED THE LE COQ SPORTIF SHIRTS, THEY REVERTED BACK TO PLAIN AND SIMPLE AND A SHIRT WORTHY OF TOTTENHAM HOTSPUR" STEVE PERRYMAN

and control the company's rivals in the sports apparel market, Horst Dassler set up Le Coq Sportif UK. The new company was to be run by Robbie Brightwell, who had previously worked for Dassler at Umbro's adidas division and, aware of the situation with Admiral and Spurs in the summer of 1980, Brightwell moved quickly.

"I called Keith Burkinshaw up out of the blue and spoke to him about what Le Coq Sportif could do in terms of a strip and generating reveunes for them", explains Brightwell. "We knew about the Admiral situation and that Umbro were going to go back in – big – for the Spurs contract. We were particularly interested in Spurs because of their profile and the fact that London would be a key area for launching the Le Coq Sportif brand."

Burkinshaw has fond memories of working closely with what he describes as "the French company". "I was really impressed by them and had a fantastic relationship with Robbie," he says.

The partnership flourished, Brightwell's Le Coq Sportif producing a series of shirts that were the epitome of early eighties football shirt chic. Plain and simple but with a bright, modern look and a touch of undoubted Spurs style, the shirts were hugely popular at the time and are still cherished today.

As Steve Perryman puts it: "Admiral pushed the boundaries maybe a little too far, in

terms of style, but then Le Coq Sportif returned it to its traditions. The players loved the Le Coq Sportif shirts, they reverted back to plain and simple and a shirt worthy of Tottenham Hotspur."

Le Coq Sportif also supplied Aston Villa in the midlands and Merseyside giants Everton. "We didn't have a big marketing budget, so by targeting the right clubs in the various different ITV regions we could maximise free exposure of the brand from television", explains Brightwell. "There was no money for advertising, taking out a back page ad in *Shoot* or *Match* magazines, but what we could do was get an action shot of Glenn Hoddle on the front cover wearing our strip featuring our logo.

"We wanted a different look for the fabric so that it would show up well on TV, especially under lights, and we put logos on the arms because more often than not the TV cameras and photographers had a side-on view, which helped generate brand exposure."

*Far left: Ricky Villa celebrates scoring the first of his two goals in the 1981 FA Cup final replay, a glorious night in the club's history accentuated by the clean, continental style of the Le Coq Sportif kit*

*Above, left: Garth Crooks shows off the manufacturer's logos on the sleeves of the away shirt, a distinctive feature of the Le Coq Sportif kits*

*Above: The Spurs shirt from 1982 onwards was the first football shirt to incorporate a 'shadow stripe' fabric*

*Left: Le Coq Sportif pioneered the production of club-related apparel*

*Above: Spurs certainly went to town at the launch of the new Hummel kit, with extensive coverage in the Spurs News*

*Right: Manager Peter Shreeve poses with Clive Allen (left) and Clive's cousin, Paul, in the new-look Hummel kit in the summer of 1985*

turn around a full set of embroidered Holsten shirts in six days before a televised game against Manchester United.

In the boardroom Spurs were also undergoing significant change, following Irving Scholar's takeover in 1982. Scholar tore up the rulebook for the conventional way to run a football club and in 1983 Tottenham Hotspur became the first club to be listed on the London Stock Exchange. Scholar wanted Spurs to be a bigger and more commercial enterprise. He envisaged the club as a broader based leisure company, exploiting the hitherto unrealised financial potential of the Tottenham Hotspur Football Club 'brand'. Key to his vision was the famous Spurs shirt and the idea that the club should be earning greater revenues from it. So when, in 1985, issues at adidas saw Horst Dassler recalled to the head office back in Germany and Robbie Brightwell leave Le Coq Sportif for pastures new, the door was opened for a 'first of its kind' deal with Danish sportswear outfit, Hummel.

Logos were also added to the the base of the numbers on the backs of the shirts, another example of Brightwell's intuition and creative instinct. And for the 1982/83 centenary season Brightwell and his team sourced a revolutionary new nylon/acetate mix material featuring 'shadow stripes', a fabric created by a supplier called Long Eaton Fabrics which was being copied by all the other football shirt manufacturers within a year.

This era of revolution in football shirt design also coincided with the introduction of sponsorship, and it was the classic Le Coq Sportif 'shadow stripe' shirts that were first adorned with a sponsor logo in December 1983. Tottenham Hotspur's first major sponsorship partnership, with beer brand Holsten, was arranged by the then promotions manager, Mike Rollo, who negotiated it with Alan Bridget, the managing director of Holsten UK, after a proposed deal with TSB didn't materialise. Spurs were relatively late to the party, finally securing a contract mid-way through the 1983/84 season and having to have Holsten logos hastily embroidered on to a set of shirts by John Metselaar's Kilburn Sports shop. John – the brother of Adrian, whose Minerva Football Company supplied match balls to Tottenham Hotspur for 29 years – had to

Hummel was originally a German company (the word 'hummel' in German means bumblebee, which explains the shape of the company's logo) which relocated to Denmark in the 1950s. Well-known for supplying kit to the Danish national team, they had started to dip their toe in the waters of the UK market by supplying teams like Leyton Orient, Norwich City and Middlesbrough with their distinctive kits adorned with their trademark chevrons.

Hummel's new arrangement with Tottenham was unique, with Spurs setting up a subsidiary company which owned the license for the sale and distribution of Hummel in the UK. The result was a revolutionary merchandising

## SPURS NOT ONLY PLAYED IN HUMMEL KIT, THEY ACTED AS THE UK DISTRIBUTOR FOR THE DANISH COMPANY

*Right: The Hummel deal enabled Spurs to distribute a large range of 'fashionable' sports and leisurewear to accompany the replica strip. This spectacular 'leisure jacket' was issued to the players for the 1987 FA Cup final with this one belonging to Tony Galvin*

*Below: Spurs distributed Hummel kit to other English clubs including Coventry, Southampton, Aston Villa and Wimbledon (below)*

operation whereby Spurs not only played in Hummel kit, they organised its sales and distribution operation as well as that of all the company's other British clubs including Aston Villa, Coventry, Southampton and Wimbledon as well as the Wales national team. But it wasn't just about the kits, the Spurs operation also distributed general Hummel sports and leisurewear. This was a whole new ball game.

Groundbreaking as the Hummel deal was – and the kits themselves were very popular – the story did not have a happy ending. The first problem Spurs encountered was the unexpectedly high cost of importing the products from their manufacturing base in Denmark. Eventually the manufacturing operation for the UK arm was moved to the north-east of England but the relationship was not improved when Scholar pointed the finger of blame for the 1987 FA Cup final wardrobe malfunction at Hummel, even though it was ultimately proven to be the club's mistake.

The major issue, however, was that Spurs' subsidiary company was ordering far more stock than was necessary

and therefore haemorrhaging cash. John Griffin, formerly of Admiral Sportswear, was brought in as managing director of the subsidiary company in 1988 to try and come up with a plan to reduce the saturated stock levels. But distribution was significantly hindered by the lack of major sports retail chains, with the likes of Olympus and Champion Sports the only ones to be found on UK high streets, leaving the sales team facing the time-consuming task of selling in to the numerous small, independent sports shops still prevalent at the time.

Scholar's desire for expansion had run into trouble. The Hummel distribution deal turned into a financial disaster which, compounded by other misadventures as well as the huge overspend on the construction of the new East Stand at White Hart Lane, very nearly brought the club to its knees. By 1990 the club was estimated to be between £18 and £23 million in debt.

Extricating the club from the deal with Hummel was going to be tricky, but it was now apparent to both parties that the arrangement was just not working. Early in 1990 Hummel's Bob Roberts met with Scholar in London where it was agreed that the contract would run for a further year, until the end of the 1990/91 season, with Spurs paying a disengagement fee.

Tottenham Hotspur's financial crisis was deepening and the Midland Bank was knocking at the door. The situation was a mess, highlighted by the fact that when Spurs visited Southampton in late December of 1990 the home match programme ran a piece about the lack of available replica kit over Christmas under the headline, "This problem has been caused by Tottenham Hotspur PLC". The article continued: "…who are not prepared to restock the Shop fully during the last year of their agreement".

And within a few months it became apparent why. After the famous 1991 FA Cup semi-final victory over rivals Arsenal at Wembley, Hummel immediately set about producing a set of new kit for the final, including match detail embroidered shirts for the showpiece occasion. But in the background, and under a veil of secrecy, Scholar was already in advanced negotiations with Peter Kenyon at Umbro with a view to signing a more traditional kit

## THE HUMMEL DISTRIBUTION DEAL CONTRIBUTED TO A FINANCIAL DISASTER THAT NEARLY BROUGHT THE CLUB TO ITS KNEES

deal for the 1991/92 season and beyond. On reaching the final, Spurs decided to write-off the contract with Hummel so that they could wear their new Umbro kit in the final, in so doing risking a hefty lawsuit from the Danish manufacturers. The first that Hummel knew about it was when the set of shirts they had prepared for Wembley were sent back to them.

And so, somewhat controversially, Tottenham Hotspur walked out at Wembley in their new Umbro shirts along with the headline-grabbing revolutionary long shorts. Justin Edinburgh, then a young full-back, remembers the whole thing well: "We'd heard rumours that there was going to be a new kit but we didn't actually see it until we got to the dressing room at the stadium. I was surprised that Terry Venables had allowed it, as players like Gazza were very superstitious and would have wanted to stick with the same Hummel kit we'd worn in the semi-final. But it was never discussed with the players and when we saw the shorts it was definitely a bit of a shock!"

Just like the Admiral, Le Coq Sportif and Hummel shirts that had gone before them, the new Umbro Spurs kit was at the forefront of the latest in football fashion and Tottenham Hotspur went into the 1990s leading the way again – although it needed the sale of Gazza to Lazio in Italy, and ultimately a takeover by Alan Sugar, to truly get the club's finances back on track.

These tough times may be but a distant memory today, but the kits the team wore during this era are amongst the best-loved of all Spurs shirts.

Gary Mabbutt, who lifted the cup for Spurs in 1991, sums it up perfectly: "I joined in 1982 and the 1980s and 1990s was the best era for Spurs shirts. There were some amazing kits in the true traditions and the colours of the club. Some seriously decent shirts."

*Above: Paul Gascoigne and Gary Lineker celebrate beating Arsenal at Wembley in the 1991 FA Cup semi-final. But when they returned for the final they were wearing a brand new Umbro kit*

*Left: The cup final shirt that never was. It was only when the match-prepared Hummel shirts were returned that the Danish company realised that Tottenham Hotspur's ninth FA Cup final appearance was not destined to be their Spurs swansong*

# HOME 1977/78

*Match worn by* JOHN PRATT

Tottenham Hotspur's drop in to the Second Division in 1977 saw a raft of changes throughout the club as Spurs took the opportunity to wipe the slate clean and go again. Probably the most noticeable change, apart from the slightly unfamiliar names of some of the visiting teams, was an innovative and daring new Admiral strip that could not fail to gain attention.

Significantly, this was the first Spurs home shirt ever produced which contained an additional embellishment to the crisp white design other than the club badge and numbers. Thankfully for the traditionalists, many of whom were surprised at the new style which they claimed polluted the pure lilywhite shirt, the colour that was added was the club's traditional navy.

The original pioneers of the late 1970s revolution in football shirt design, driven by the potential commercial gold mine of the replica shirt market, Admiral's bold and revolutionary approach completely changed the perception of what a football shirt could and should look like.

The primary features that made the radical new Spurs Admiral shirt so different were the navy v-neck of the collar and taping down the arms, both of which were branded with multiple Admiral logos. A large Admiral logo also appeared on the right breast of the shirt. Another radical change was the introduction of a large white winged collar, which replaced the crew-necked design that had been a feature of the club's shirts for the last 15 years. Navy blue contrasting cuffs also made their first ever appearance on a Spurs home shirt. The large embroidered cockerel-and-ball club crest now incorporated a Victorian-style football on which the cockerel stood, rather than the panelled ball seen on its predecessor.

The kit was unveiled with surprisingly little fanfare, the club announcing its arrival with a small piece in the programme for the opening match of the season against Sheffield United.

*The new Admiral shirt signalled a turn in fortunes for Spurs as they returned to the top flight with John Pratt – another home-grown and loyal servant of the club – ever-present in this No.7 shirt*

# HOME 1978/79

*Match worn by* GLENN HODDLE

Promotion back to Division One quietened some of the dissenting voices concerning the revolutionary Admiral design, but perhaps the biggest factor in the overwhelming acceptance of the kit – and what made the Spurs shirt one of the most fashionable in the game – was the sensational arrival of two Argentinian World Cup winners.

When Ossie Ardiles and Ricky Villa were unveiled at White Hart Lane in their pristine full Admiral strips and then received an unprecedented ticker-tape welcome when they ran out in it for their first home game, it provided some of the most iconic images of the 1970s… not just of Spurs but of English football in general.

The actual shirt design for the second Admiral season was the same as the previous season's, but with one subtle difference. The number style changed from the narrow font seen on the 1977/78 shirt to a thicker, solid block style. This was an Admiral design change across their full range of shirts for its various teams and makes identifying rare Spurs shirts that were worn during the Second Division campaign a relatively straightforward process.

Although the shirt is essentially a template design that was rolled out across a number of clubs, the white and navy colour combination was unique to Tottenham in the Admiral catalogue.

By this time the introduction of man-made fibres was becoming the norm, and although the club's first replica shirts were made from nylon, those worn by the players continued to be made in the softer natural fibres of cotton.

Now establishing himself in the side alongside Ardiles was home-grown talent Glenn Hoddle, who during the 1978/79 season made the No.4 shirt his own. But as the new Spurs team increasingly began to be built around him, Hoddle would later adopt the totemic No.10 on the back of his shirt.

*Above: Glenn Hoddle in action during the 1978/79 campaign, which saw him emerge as a potential star of the future*

*Above: The No.4 on this shirt – unusual in that Hoddle is generally associated with the No.10 – is in the solid block font adopted in Admiral's second season*

# AWAY 1977-80

*Match worn by* CHRIS JONES

This typically bold Admiral design was worn for all of the three seasons that Spurs were contracted to the Leicestershire-based kit supplier.

The highly distinctive shirt was produced in the familiar shade of yellow that had featured on all the club's recent change shirts and had a large, winged navy collar and an Admiral-branded v-neck, similar to the corresponding home shirt, as well as navy cuffs. But the distinguishing features that made this very popular shirt stand out were the unique navy lapel-like half-braces descending from each shoulder.

The left brace always contained a large club crest in white, and originally the Admiral logo in yellow and blue appeared within the right brace as it does on the shirt pictured. However, there were inconsistencies in Admiral's production process that meant that on certain runs of kit the company's logo appeared not on the brace itself but just inside. This occurred initially on the first long-sleeved versions but later appeared on short-sleeved shirts too. Another variation is that some shirts featured the white and blue Admiral logo as seen on the home shirt rather than the yellow and blue version. Over the years this has caused considerable confusion, leading some to believe that there were two different versions of the same Admiral away shirt when in fact the position and colour of the company's logo are the only differences.

On the shirt pictured here the thick block font number and the yellow and blue Admiral logo dates the shirt to the 1979/80 season, during which the regular incumbent of the No.8 jersey was centre-forward Chris Jones.

*Above: Ossie Ardiles, Ricky Villa, Terry Yorath and Glenn Hoddle – in his trademark smaller shorts – form a slightly apprehensive-looking wall*

*Above: Earlier versions of this shirt carried a white, rather than yellow, Admiral logo*

# HOME 1979–PRE-SEASON 1980

*Match worn by* OSSIE ARDILES

Pre-season 1980 was one of heightened expectation at White Hart Lane because of the exciting and improving squad that Keith Burkinshaw had assembled, but sadly for many it was to prove Admiral's final act in the Spurs shirt story. The company's dramatic entry into the kit market burned brightly but briefly, their deal with Tottenham Hotspur coming to an abrupt end just after they called in the receivers in the summer of 1980.

This left Spurs with a serious problem: the need to find a brand-new kit supplier at very short notice. While they searched for a new supplier, the club had no option other than to play all six of their pre-season matches in the previous season's Admiral strips.

Worn by Ossie Ardiles in the pre-season friendly against Rangers at Ibrox on 4 August 1980 – and swapped afterwards with Rangers' Colin Jackson – the shirt pictured is therefore one of the last of the Spurs Admiral shirts ever to see action. It is extremely rare to be able to have such game-specific detail for a shirt of this period because kit was continually used over the course of the season and players were prohibited from swapping.

Still fondly remembered to this day, the Admiral Spurs shirt was the last Spurs home shirt to be worn for three full seasons. The relationship came to an end just as the Spurs side was blossoming into one of the finest teams in the land, making the club a highly attractive potential partner for any new kit supplier.

*Ossie Ardiles in action against Birmingham during the 1979/80 season. This was the last campaign when the Admiral shirt was worn, although it did make an appearance during the following pre-season*

# HOME 1980-82

*Match worn by* STEVE ARCHIBALD

In fashion terms at least, the 1980s started off with a bang for Tottenham Hotspur. The sudden demise of Admiral in the summer of 1980 meant that for the start of the 1980/81 season Spurs players ran out wearing a new supplier's kit and a brand-new shirt design for the season opener at White Hart Lane against Nottingham Forest (having played the whole of pre-season in the old Admiral strip). The UK arm of French sports apparel brand Le Coq Sportif acted quickly and negotiated the switch, signalling the start of a new era which would turn out to be one of the most exciting in the club's history.

Le Coq Sportif UK had entered the British football market in 1978 with Derby County, but the size and prestige of Spurs dramatically increased their brand exposure and they would go on to produce some memorable shirts that were worn on some truly momentous occasions.

The first Le Coq Sportif home shirt was the first Spurs shirt to have the newly fashionable shiny fabric look, made possible by recent advances in man-made fibre technology. Notable for its classic simplicity in comparison to its heavily branded Admiral predecessor, the pure white template was embellished with a narrow navy trim on the v-neck and cuffs. The crest was moved to the centre of the shirt and the manufacturer's logos added to each sleeve, which maximised the visibility of the company's branding and gave the jersey a fresh, continental feel.

Steve Archibald's big-money arrival in the summer of 1980 was seen as a statement of intent by Spurs. The Scot is remembered by fans as a wearer of long-sleeved shirts, and he revealed in a *Shoot* magazine interview a few years after joining Spurs that his preference for long sleeves was one of the primary reasons he had joined his first Scottish club, Clyde.

"The other option, East Stirling, only had short-sleeved shirts and I didn't like their black and white hoop colours," he said.

*Above: Steve Archibald in action, wearing – as ever – long sleeves*

*Right: Cloth stich-applied numbers were used for the 1980/81 season, as seen on this Tony Galvin shirt*

*Top right: Le Coq Sportif changed the number design for the 1981 FA Cup final and this new shadow block style was used during the following season*

# AWAY 1980-82

*Match shirt of* PAUL PRICE *and* GRAHAM ROBERTS

Le Coq Sportif's first Tottenham away shirt was equally as tasteful and stylish as its home counterpart.

Deep yellow in colour, the design included two epaulette-effect navy panels on the shoulders and sported a plain, non-contrasting v-neck. Similar to the home shirt, it boasted a centrally placed, embroidered crest and Le Coq Sportif logos located on the outside of each sleeve, again to achieve maximum brand exposure.

The away jersey was made from the same nylon/acetate material mix as the home shirt, giving it a silky, shiny appearance. The material incorporated an early example of moisture-wicking technology, and brushed back nylon gave the inside of the shirt a soft, fluffy feel and helped it absorb sweat.

Over the course of its initial two-season lifetime, this attractive design was actually worn on 21 occasions: 10 times in 1980/81, nine in 1981/82, plus most notably in the two FA Cup final matches at the end of that season. It was also twice dusted down for use as an emergency third shirt in the 1983/84 season – with the addition of then sponsor Holsten's logo – for the 1984 UEFA Cup semi-final first leg away tie against Hajduk Split on 11 April, and then nearly three weeks later the same set of shirts was worn for a league clash with Queens Park Rangers. These shirts carried the smaller version of the sponsor logo to comply with UEFA regulations.

Regular wearers of the yellow No.4 shirt in 1981/82 were Graham Roberts and Welsh international Paul Price, who put pressure on Roberts and Paul Miller for their centre-half places and benefited from Roberts' occasional selection in midfield.

*Above: Ossie Ardiles majestically plies his craft in the stylish yellow Le Coq Sportif away kit against Southampton*

*Right: As with the home shirt, the Le Coq Sportif branding was increased for the shirt's second season – the 1981/82 campaign – with the addition of shadow block numbers incorporating the manufacturer's logo*

# FA CUP FINAL 1981

*Match worn by* STEVE PERRYMAN

The 100th FA Cup competition delivered a first trophy for the great Tottenham team of the era, and Perryman, Hoddle, Ardiles and co. fulfilled 'Ossies' Dream' of gracing the hallowed Wembley turf in Le Coq Sportif's first cup final version of the famous lilywhite jersey.

For the final against Manchester City, the club's relatively new kit manufacturer provided a set of home shirts adorned with the now familiar cup final embroidery – 'FA CUP FINAL' and 'WEMBLEY 1981' over two lines – and complete with a sizeable Le Coq Sportif logo embroided on each arm.

What was new, however, were the numbers, which were modern-looking and Le Coq Sportif-designed in a shadow block font. Unlike the more traditional-style sewn-on cloth numbers that had been used all season until now, these were created by placing a stencil on the shirt through which glue was applied before flock (essentially tiny pieces of felt) was sprayed on to the glue.

The shirt featured here is unusual not because of the new style of number, more the digit itself. Traditionally and throughout the season Steve Perryman wore the No.6 shirt, but for the 1981 occasion he led the team out in an unfamiliar jersey.

"It was all because of a mistake in the programme," explains Perryman. "When we got to Wembley, Johnny Wallis pointed out that in it I was listed as No.5, which was usually Ricky Villa's number, with Ricky at No.6, which was mine. I had a quick chat with Ricky and as captain I made the decision that we'd go with what was in the programme so that's why I wore 5 and Ricky wore 6."

The programme mix-up may stem from the first semi-final against Wolves when Perryman also wore No.5 and Villa No.6, quite possibly because of a similar error.

As all Tottenham supporters of a certain vintage are aware, the first match – which ended in a 1-1 draw – was a massive disappointment. And just like the Spurs team, the cup final shirts massively underperformed in the wash the following day...

*Above: Spurs skipper Steve Perryman clashes with Manchester City's Kevin Reeves during the 1981 FA Cup final*

*Right: The match programme for the final listed Perryman and Villa in unfamiliar numbers*

*Above: White Le Coq Sportif logos were heat-applied to the base of each number, with the overall effect being a very early example of using shirt numbers for manufacturer branding*

**TOTTENHAM HOTSPUR**

(Colours: White Shirts, Dark Blue Shorts, White Stockings)

1. MILIJA ALEKSIC
2. CHRIS HUGHTON
3. PAUL MILLER
4. GRAHAM ROBERTS
5. STEVE PERRYMAN (Captain)
6. RICARDO VILLA
7. OSVALDO ARDILES
8. STEVE ARCHIBALD
9. TONY GALVIN
10. GLENN HODDLE
11. GARTH CROOKS

Substitute: GARRY BROOKE

Manager: KEITH BURKINSHAW

# FA CUP FINAL REPLAY 1981

*Match worn by* RICKY VILLA

Worn by Ricky Villa as he went on his famous mazy run through the Manchester City defence before slotting the ball under keeper Joe Corrigan to score the greatest-ever Wembley FA Cup final goal, this shirt is perhaps the most famous Spurs jersey of them all.

Villa had been extremely disappointed with his performance in the first game, trudging round the Wembley pitch in the No.6 shirt after being substituted. But not only was he picked for the replay, he was back in his more familiar No.5 shirt. As Steve Perryman explains: "After things didn't go right in the first game, especially for Ricky, I decided we'd go back to our usual numbers even though the programme still had me listed at 5 and him at 6."

However, the actual shirts they wore for the dramatic 3-2 victory – one of the most famous Spurs nights of them all – were not the same ones they'd worn in the first match. Those had been gathered up by Johnny Wallis after the game and sent straight back to White Hart Lane to be washed and prepared for the replay, scheduled for five days later. But when laundry lady Sylvie Webb removed them from the wash the following day she noticed straight away there was a problem – the new numbers had spoiled.

"They were damaged – cracked and badly faded in places," she remembers. "There's no way a Spurs team could have run out at Wembley in them."

Webb alerted Keith Burkinshaw to the issue and the Spurs manager, having sworn her to secrecy, immediately phoned Le Coq Sportif head Robbie Brightwell who was preparing to go on holiday. Brightwell arranged for company representatives to visit White Hart Lane the following day, and in time for the Thursday evening replay two new sets of FA Cup final shirts had arrived – this time with the cloth, stich-applied numbers that had been worn all season up to the final.

And over the course of the close season Le Coq Sportif set about refining their flock application techniques so that their shadow block numbers could withstand the rigours of Sylvie Webb's industrial washing machine.

*Changing back to his usual No.5 shirt for the 1981 FA Cup final replay – for which he will forever be remembered – clearly had a galvanising effect on Ricky Villa*

# FA CUP FINAL 1981

Kit man Johnny Wallis threw out the set of damaged shirts from the first match, except for three which were held back by Sylvie Webb to assist Le Coq Sportif in improving their flock application technique for their new style numbers.

One of these was Steve Perryman's unusual No.5 shirt, which was never discarded and happily survives to this day

Ricky Villa's shirt from the replay, complete with its traditional cloth stitched No.5 following the problems with the new Le Coq Sportif numbers on the first set of shirts

# LEAGUE CUP FINAL 1982

*Match worn by* CHRIS HUGHTON

With the previous season's FA Cup freshly installed in the trophy cabinet at White Hart Lane, Keith Burkinshaw's Spurs reached Wembley again in March 1982. It meant Le Coq Sportif's celebrated first Spurs home jersey would be worn at Wembley for the fourth time in less than two years (it had also been worn in the Charity Shield season opener against Aston Villa, who also wore Le Coq Sportif kit). No wonder this shirt is so fondly remembered, although on this occasion there was disappointment for Tottenham – who were challenging on four fronts during a hectic 1981/82 season – at the hands of then mighty Liverpool.

For the match, a set of home shirts was produced with the match details appearing below the cockerel-and-ball crest as they had for the 1981 FA Cup final, but this time printed in felt rather than embroidered. As a consequence of this several of the surviving shirts from this match are missing some of the letters, which have fallen off over time. The shirt featured here is the short-sleeved version worn by left-back Chris Hughton.

The numbers used for the final were the shadow block version in flock that included the Le Coq Sportif logo at the base. To meet Football League regulations for the final, the company's sleeve logos had to be smaller than the standard embroidered versions on Spurs' league shirts. These were also done in felt, like the match details, for ease of manufacturing.

Tottenham started the game brightly in the familiar Wembley setting, taking an early lead through Steve Archibald, and produced a sterling performance against a battle-hardened Liverpool, the dominant team of the era. However, it wasn't to be and Liverpool equalised late on and added two goals in extra-time to confirm victory over a clearly exhausted Spurs side.

Five days after the final, a spare set of these shirts – complete with the cup final detailing – was worn in the European Cup Winners' Cup quarter-final second leg match away to Eintracht Frankfurt.

*Chris Hughton goes past Liverpool's Mark Lawrenson during the 1982 League Cup final*

# FA CUP FINAL 1982

*Match worn by* GARTH CROOKS

Spurs found themselves back at Wembley in May 1982, attempting to retain the trophy just as they had 20 years previously in the season after winning the famous Double.

Their opponents on this occasion were London rivals QPR, and with both teams' first-choice kits being blue and white a coin toss was required to determine who would get first choice of colours. QPR won the toss so Spurs elected to wear their yellow away strip. Rangers then chose to use the 'lucky' red and black away kit that they had worn in their semi-final victory over West Brom.

A set of away shirts were prepared by Le Coq Sportif, with the match detail 'FA CUP FINAL WEMBLEY 1982' embroidered beneath the central crest over three lines. Le Coq Sportif were again surprisingly allowed their double sleeve branding for the showpiece occasion, as well as their logos at the base of the numbers.

Like the previous season, the final went to a replay and the same set of shirts was worn for the second match that was played just five days later.

The No.11 shirt was worn in both matches by Garth Crooks, who arrived from Stoke City in August 1980 to form a thrillingly effective strike pairing with Steve Archibald. Crooks provided an excellent goal return during his time at Spurs; 22 goals in his debut season and 75 in total over a five-year period at the club.

While Crooks did not get on the scoresheet this time, he picked up his second FA Cup winners' medal in successive years. After a dour draw in the first game, Hoddle gave Spurs the advantage from the penalty spot in the replay. And while Spurs were second best for much of the match, they had just enough to hold off their Second Division opponents to lift the trophy and become the first team to retain the FA Cup since the great Bill Nicholson's Spurs side of the 1960s.

*Garth Crooks rises above the QPR defence during the 1982 FA Cup final. The same shirts were used for the replay five days later*

# HOME CENTENARY 1982/83

## *Match shirt of* STEVE PERRYMAN

Tottenham Hotspur Football Club celebrated its 100th birthday in 1982, and to mark the centenary Le Coq Sportif produced three groundbreaking shirts that are amongst the most stylish and celebrated of all Spurs jerseys.

Following the back-to-back FA Cup wins of 1981 and 1982, going into their centenary season Tottenham were firmly positioned as one of the top English clubs both on and off the pitch. And, in keeping with the times as well as the stature of Spurs, Le Coq Sportif produced a superb set of shirts featuring a revolutionary 'shadow stripe' effect never before seen on an English club shirt. It was appropriately dynamic and seemed to symbolise a desire to look forward to greater successes rather than harking back to past glories.

The 'shadow stripe' effect – a matt-and-gloss-striped fabric – appeared on all three shirts; a classic white home number, a 'powder blue' away shirt and a sleek pale yellow third shirt that was never available to buy as a replica.

On the prototype samples initially produced by Le Coq Sportif the crest appeared, as it had on the company's previous designs, in the centre of the chest. However, Spurs requested that for this landmark season it revert to its more traditional position on the left breast. And on all three of the centenary shirt designs it appeared with the text 'CENTENARY YEAR' embroidered in an arc above it, with the years '1882' and '1982' positioned either side of the cockerel and ball and the words 'TOTTENHAM HOTSPUR' contained in a scroll below.

The position of the crest meant that for balance the manufacturer's logo moved to the right breast and there were no Le Coq Sportif logos on the sleeves.

The yellow third shirt was specifically produced to be worn in just one game, a friendly away at Bristol Rovers in April 1983 which marked the home side's own centenary. Given these were the days long before highlights of every game were shown on television, many supporters were not even aware of this shirt's existence.

*Above: In keeping with the importance of the season of celebrations, the number style on all three centenary shirts reverted to the more traditional cloth variety – without Le Coq Sportif branding – which were stitched on to the shirts*

*Left: Legendary Spurs skipper Steve Perryman leads the way in the commemorative centenary shirt*

# AWAY CENTENARY 1982/83

*Match worn by* OSSIE ARDILES

*A shirt worn by Ossie Ardiles in a friendly away to Luton following his return to Spurs after the Falklands War*

# THIRD CENTENARY 1982/83

*Match worn by* GLENN HODDLE

This shirt was worn by Glenn Hoddle in the match to celebrate Bristol Rovers' centenary and is the only known surviving example of this jersey, which was only used in this one game

# HOME 1983-85

*Match worn by* TONY GALVIN

The template created for the club's magnificent centenary shirt continued to do sterling service after the 100th birthday celebrations had died down, although for the 1983/84 season the badge was moved back to the centre of the chest, returning to the stylish, continental feel.

A more noticeable change for this season was the introduction of a shirt sponsor. Shirt sponsorship was nothing new in football, especially abroad. In England, Kettering Town had unsuccessfully challenged the FA's strict rules in 1976 when they became the first English team to wear sponsored shirts emblazoned with 'Kettering Tyres'. In 1977 Hibernian sported the logo of their kit manufacturer, Bukta, on their shirts, causing a blackout of televised football in Scotland, and by 1979 sponsored shirts were allowed in non-televised games in the Football League. In 1983 the broadcasters finally relented and allowed teams to wear sponsors' logos, albeit reduced in size by 50 per cent, in games on television.

For such a commercially pioneering club, Spurs took a long time to join the party. It should be remembered that there was historical context, however, with the club having refused to have advertising hoardings at White Hart Lane for decades. But finally, after the start of the 1983/84 season, Spurs struck a deal with the beer brand Holsten, beginning a long and fondly remembered association between the two parties.

The watershed moment came on 16 December 1983 when Spurs travelled to Manchester United for the first-ever live league match televised in full by the BBC and fully embroidered Holsten logos appeared on the lilywhite shirts for the very first time.

The shirt pictured is one prepared for a televised game with the reduced-size logo.

*Left: Tony Galvin is pictured wearing the version of the shirt with the larger Holsten logo*

*Below left: The European version of this shirt saw the club crest moved back to the left breast, with a single Le Coq Sportif logo appearing on the right breast as UEFA rules stipulated that only one manufacturer's logo was permitted. These regulations also meant that the Le Coq Sportif logo at the base of the shirt numbers could not be displayed – so these were masked by a piece of cloth*

# AWAY 1983-85

*Match worn by* MARK FALCO

The 1983–85 powder blue away shirt was exactly the same design as the popular jersey from the previous season's centenary celebrations, except that the crest was moved back to the centre of the jersey with Le Coq Sportif logos returning to their more familiar position on the sleeves.

This was also the first Spurs away shirt to carry a sponsor logo, with Holsten coming on board in December 1983, and the beer brand's logo first appeared on the away shirt for the visit to Fulham in the FA Cup in January 1984.

Most of the shirts of this style produced for Spurs featured the smaller, television-friendly Holsten logo which makes the jersey featured here – with its full-size branding only for use in non-televised matches – an extremely rare and collectible example.

The players' shirts from this period are easily distinguishable from the replica versions that were sold in the Spurs Shop by the fact that the crest and Le Coq Sportif logos on the former were embroidered rather than heat-pressed in felt. The team shirts also sported new-style solid block numbers applied in flock, which commonly, although not always, featured Le Coq Sportif logos in the base of each digit.

This shirt style was worn four times during the 1983/84 season, twice with and twice without Holsten logos, and six times the following season, five times in the league and once against Real Madrid in the UEFA Cup.

On two occasions in April 1984 – against Queens Park Rangers and later Hajduk Split in the UEFA Cup – the shirt was not deemed suitable as an alternative to the white home jersey (because both opponents played in blue and white) and yellow 1980–82 jerseys, with added Holsten logos, were worn.

*Above: Mark Falco gets his shot away despite the best efforts of Paul Parker during the 1984 FA Cup clash between Spurs and Fulham*

*Left: Before the Holsten sponsorship deal was signed, the shirt was worn – away to Stoke and Luton in late 1983 – without sponsor logos*

# UEFA CUP HOME 1983/84

*Match worn by* GARY O'REILLY

For Tottenham's ultimately glorious 1983/84 UEFA Cup campaign, competition regulations necessitated the production of a bespoke shirt.

Because European football's governing body's rules stipulated that only one manufacturer's logo was allowed, Le Coq Sportif reconfigured the standard home shirt. As they had done with the centenary shirts, the crest was moved to the left breast and a single manufacturer's logo was placed on the right. Unlike the domestic shirt, no logos appeared on the sleeves.

And, perhaps because the shirts would only be used in Europe, Spurs made the decision to adorn them with bespoke competition-specific embroidery. Unfortunately, however, in the first batch of shirts a mistake occurred with the lettering reading 'E.U.F.A. 1983–84' rather than 'U.E.F.A.'.

This typographical error did not go unnoticed, with *Shoot* gleefully pointing it out under the heading "Oops!", with the magazine suggesting that someone at the club had 'goofed'. "Spelling obviously isn't their strong point," joked the article. But in fact the error had occurred at Kilburn Sports, where the embroidery was done

Rectified on the shirts worn from the quarter-finals onwards, this mistake massively increases the rarity and collectability of the jerseys which were used in the first three rounds of the competition – against Drogheda United of Ireland, Feyenoord and Bayern Munich.

The shirt featured here was worn by Gary O'Reilly against the might Bayern Munich on 7 December 1983, when he came on as a substitute in the 2-0 third round second leg victory to replace Chris Hughton.

The Holsten logo also did not appear on this shirt until the later rounds, after the beer brand sponsored the home leg of the Bayern Munich tie, with the sponsorship deal only being sealed towards the end of 1983.

Top: Steve Archibald in the thick of the action against Bayern Munich

Above: The presence of 'E.U.F.A.' instead of 'U.E.F.A.' on Spurs' European shirts was spotted by Shoot magazine

Right: Le Coq Sportif bent the UEFA rules on the number of manufacturer logos allowed on shirts by using numbers featuring their branding, although these were covered up for the later rounds

# UEFA CUP AWAY 1983/84

*Match worn by* PAUL MILLER

Another extremely rare and highly prized jersey, the away shirt produced for the 1983/84 UEFA Cup campaign was worn on just two occasions – against Austria Vienna in the quarter-final second leg and in the first leg of the final away to Anderlecht.

Reconfigured as per the home shirt – with the cockerel-and-ball crest over the left breast and a single Le Coq Sportif logo on the right, with none appearing on the sleeves – the jersey also featured the bespoke competition embroidery but this time with 'U.E.F.A.' spelt correctly.

Another difference from its home equivalent from the early rounds was that the Holsten logo now appeared, albeit in the smaller size to conform with UEFA (rather than television) regulations. In addition, the previously visible Le Coq Sportif logos in the base of the cloth stitched numbers were blocked out with patches of navy cloth, no doubt having been brought to the attention of the competition's administrators.

The long-sleeved shirt featured here was worn by stalwart defender Paul Miller in the 2-2 quarter-final second leg draw with Austria Vienna. Like most of the rest of the team, Miller wore short sleeves in the first leg of the final – in which he scored Tottenham's only goal in the 1-1 draw – although unlike the shirts for the second leg the word 'FINAL' was not added to the embroidery located beneath the crest.

*Left: Tony Galvin is pictured in the short-sleeved version of this shirt which was used during the first leg of the final away to Anderlecht*

*Below: A close-up of the base of the No.5 shows how cloth patches were used to cover up the Le Coq Sportif logos for European competition*

# UEFA CUP FINAL 2nd LEG 1984

### *Match worn by* GRAHAM ROBERTS

One of the most iconic shirts from one of Tottenham Hotspur's most iconic games, Graham Roberts' jersey from the glorious UEFA Cup victory in front of a packed and raucous White Hart Lane is more than a football shirt, it is a monument to Keith Burkinshaw's great team and to the wearer himself who drove Spurs forward when all looked lost on one of the club's greatest and most famous nights.

Having taken over the captain's armband for the second leg of the final against Anderlecht in the absence of suspended club captain Steve Perryman, Roberts pulled on the UEFA Cup version of the club's home jersey – albeit with the word 'FINAL' added on a single line below the competition embroidery in a slightly different font and a lighter shade of navy – and ran himself into the ground in pursuit of victory.

With Spurs losing 1-0 on the night, 2-1 down on aggregate and facing defeat, in the 84th minute Roberts powered into the crowded Anderlecht box, calmly controlled Micky Hazard's cross on his chest, allowed the ball to drop before his right foot gently nudged the ball past the stranded opposition goalkeeper and into the net. It prompted one of the loudest roars ever heard at the old stadium – a scream of celebration, relief, joy and renewed optimism. The scorer careered away in open-mouthed delight, White Hart Lane a cacophony of noise and terrace-shuddering excitement.

The goal took the match into extra-time and then penalties, where Tony Parks proved to be the ultimate hero, but Roberts – in this mud-stained, sweat-soaked shirt – lifted the trophy in front of the heaving, joyous Shelf on this night of all nights.

The only other distinguishing feature of this famous shirt is the large block number which did not include a Le Coq Sportif logo so did not require a covering patch.

*Left: Graham Roberts wheels away in celebration following his crucial 84th-minute goal against Anderlecht in the second leg of the 1984 UEFA Cup final at White Hart Lane*

*Right: After the game Roberts did not swap shirts but in 1994 his historic No.4 jersey was sold at auction, along with his winners' medal*

*Below, left: The difference in embroidery styles shows that the word 'FINAL' was added to an older set of shirts*

U.E.F.A. 1983-84
FINAL

HOLSTEN

# HOME 1985-87

*Match worn by* DAVID LEWORTHY

In 1985, Tottenham Hotspur secured the licensing and UK distribution rights for Danish sportswear company Hummel as part of chairman Irving Scholar's grand plan to increase the club's commercial operation and bring in increased revenue.

The first Hummel shirt was unveiled in the summer of 1985 to great fanfare, with a kit launch at White Hart Lane at which Gary Mabbutt and Mark Falco posed for promotional photographs in the new home and away kits on the catwalk alongside professional models.

The word 'Hummel' is actually the German word for bumblebee (the company was originally German) and the new shirt was certainly busy. Now considered one of the all-time – if not *the* all-time – classic Tottenham Hotspur shirts, the initial reaction was very mixed with many traditionalists arguing that the sacred lilywhite shirt was being tarnished by the diagonal pinstripes and chevron patterns that characterised the company's shirts.

In addition to the daring overall design, the bold decision by Hummel to go with white shorts, hitherto almost exclusively used for European competition or in the event of colour a clash, embodied abrupt change and the tearing up of tradition.

This shirt is the first Spurs example of the new trend of what is known as dye-sublimation printing, which means the use of heat-sensitive inks combined with polyester allowing badges, logos and design features to be contained within the structure of the material rather than being printed or flocked (to avoid fading and cracking).

The No.12 shirt pictured is an example of the earliest incarnation of the Hummel design, which didn't include these techniques. Due to the rush to produce shirts in time for pre-season, those worn at the start of the campaign featured an embroided club crest, Hummel wordmark and full-stitched Holsten logo as well as old Le Coq Sportif stitch-applied cloth numbers (with their logos masked) which makes surviving examples extremely rare.

*Above and right: This first version of the shirt was worn all the way through pre-season, including testimonials for Glenn Hoddle and Ossie Ardiles (when it was worn by Diego Maradona). The most likely incumbent of this No.12 jersey was new signing David Leworthy*

*Right: A later long-sleeved version of the jersey shows how a shade of lilac was used for the trademark Hummel chevrons on some shirts, and the fact that the sublimated manufacturer's logo and the club crest were moved higher up the left side of the chest*

# AWAY 1985-88

*Match worn by* GLENN HODDLE

In parallel with a growing trend for more adventurous football shirt designs throughout the English game, the animated reaction to Hummel's initial foray into the world of the Spurs shirt accelerated the pace of sartorial change at White Hart Lane. For the next few years a range of distinctive shirts were produced with increasing frequency.

Hummel went to town with this 'jacquard' design for their first Spurs away shirt, launched at the same time as the home shirt. Intricately detailed, it boasted diagonal stripes in two shades of light blue – separated by alternating white and navy pinstripes – and chevron taping down the sleeves picked out in white.

The shirt had a non-contrasting v-neck collar and cuffs, and stitch-applied cloth block font numbers in royal blue (as seen on the home shirt in pre-season) were used throughout the lifetime of this jersey.

Throughout pre-season in 1985, as with the home shirt, the club crest, Hummel and Holsten logos were all embroidered. Once the league campaign started the shirts had a vinyl printed Holsten logo, as seen on this Glenn Hoddle shirt that was worn against Luton on their plastic pitch on 28 March 1987. This shirt, and the accompanying alternative navy away shirt, never incorporated the sublimated design technique seen on the home shirt.

The shirt was worn by Hoddle in characteristic style – long and untucked, although he would occasionally tuck the back of the shirt in. Hoddle usually opted for long sleeves, although at either end of the season when the weather was warmer he would sometimes elect to sport short sleeves.

*The great Glenn Hoddle wearing the early version of the shirt with the Hummel and Holsten logos embroidered*

# HOME 1986/87

*Match worn by* RICHARD GOUGH

On the opening day of the 1985/86 season, a new version of Hummel's first shirt was worn, which had the club crest and Hummel and Holsten logos – as well as the player numbers – all sublimated within the shirt fabric.

The most noticeable development, however, was that the club crest (significantly smaller than the previous embroidered edition) and Hummel logos were now higher up on each side of the chest. This was a conscious decision taken to make the Hummel branding more visible. The new sublimated numbers on this updated version appeared in a squared-off, digital-style font, with a narrow outline around each numeral and the addition of the Hummel bumblebee logo in the base.

No doubt one of the reasons for the enduring popularity of this shirt is that it was worn during a fantastic season for the club. The 1986/87 campaign saw Spurs fighting on three fronts for most of the season, with Clive Allen famously scoring 49 goals.

The shirt pictured was worn by skipper Richard Gough in the penultimate league game of the season, away to Watford who had Spurs old boy Mark Falco leading the line. During the highly physical encounter Falco and Gough repeatedly clashed, with the resulting tear appearing down the front of Gough's shirt.

"I have a picture of me in this shirt at home," says Gough. "I always believed it was from the FA Cup final, but of course it has Holsten on it so it can't be. I don't remember the exact incident with Mark when the shirt got ripped, but I do recall the tough battle I had with him all game."

After the match the shirt was past the point of repair and would have been thrown away, but kit man Johnny Wallis asked laundry lady Sylvie Webb if her son, Colin, would like it as a souvenir and thus it just avoided ending up in the 'The Wal's' bin.

*Above: Unlike the early versions, from the start of the 1985/86 season the club crest, Holsten logo, trim and new-style player numbers were sublimated into the fabric in either blue or a shade of lilac*

*Left: Richard Gough plays on against Watford having had his shirt ripped during a clash with ex-Spurs hero Mark Falco*

# THIRD 1986-89

*Match worn by* GLENN HODDLE

This striking jersey was originally launched as an alternative away shirt and not marketed as a third shirt. But it officially became the third shirt for the 1987/88 season and was retained for the season after that, although in fact it was never worn during that campaign.

The design of the shirt was fundamentally the same as the sky blue away shirt, but the colour scheme was both striking and surprising. Two-tone diagonal navy blue stripes were laced with diagonal pinstripes of sky blue and white and the white contrasting v-neck and cuffs were highlighted with a single navy blue stripe. Unusually for a Hummel shirt at this time, there was no chevron taping down the sleeves.

The colour choice was surprising because dark coloured shirts, specifically navy, had technically been banned by the Football League since 1969 to avoid kits clashing with the black uniforms of the match officials. If they were in contravention of any rules, the club was never sanctioned for their choice of colour. However it did cause an issue for one particular game. Prior to the away match at Coventry on 28 December 1986, the referee decided that the dark blue shirts clashed with the home side's blue-and-white stripes, forcing Spurs to play in the hosts' yellow change shirts. Spurs lost 4-3 to dent their title challenge.

Perhaps because of this issue with the dark colour and particularly the clash with the officials' uniforms, the shirt was only ever worn on three occasions during its three-season lifespan. The first time was away against QPR in 1986/87, and it was then worn twice the following season, firstly on the opening day of the 1987/88 season against Spurs' recent cup conquerors Coventry City – which is why it is wrongly assumed by many to have been the first-choice away kit for that season – and then away to Sheffield Wednesday.

This was another popular shirt in terms of replica shirt sales, but it proved to have very little functional use as a match shirt.

*Glenn Hoddle in action – with his shorts barely visible as was his style – away to QPR in October 1986, one of only three competitive outings when this kit was worn*

# FA CUP FINAL 1987

The 1987 FA Cup final provided the setting for one of the most famous and bizarre stories in the history of the showpiece final, when a kit mix-up ended up overshadowing the match itself. Following a series of unique and unfortunate circumstances that are hard to believe, half of the shirts worn by the Spurs team in the final – beamed out to a global television audience of around 100 million – featured the logo of their sponsor, Holsten, while the other half didn't.

This unprecedented situation, which caused the club serious embarrassment and resulted in a huge fallout within the structure of the club management and the kit room, has been the subject of numerous conspiracy theories and flawed explanations. This, however, is the real story.

Immediately after their semi-final victory over Watford and after discussions with kit manufacturer Hummel, it was decided that Spurs would request permission to wear next season's new home kit at Wembley in the event that they won the toss to allow them to wear their home colours. This had to be sanctioned by the FA and agreed with their opponents for the final, Coventry City, which was done on the condition that Spurs would wear white shorts (the new kit would see a return to navy shorts) as this was the designated first-choice colour for the 1986/87 season. Having duly won the coin toss, Spurs proceeded with the plan, and Coventry elected to wear their blue-and-white-striped home shirts but with navy shorts rather than their usual white so as not to clash.

In the weeks leading up to the final, the club were supplied with six full sets of the new kit by Hummel. Four of these included the logo of sponsors Holsten across the chest, but two sets of the shirts were unbranded because they had been ordered for the youth team to use in an end of season tournament in Germany. At the time Spurs' policy was not to carry the name of their sponsor on their youth team's shirts because of the alcoholic nature of its product.

The shirts were sent to club secretary Peter Day,

who was tasked with organising the bespoke cup final embroidery, and the box was sitting in his office when he received a phonecall from the FA informing him that, with a huge global television audience from countries of all different cultures, potential alcohol advertising issues meant that Spurs might not be allowed to have 'Holsten' on their shirts for the final. This was the first FA Cup final where a team with an alcoholic sponsor was due to appear.

As he already had two sets of unbranded shirts fortunately sitting in his office, Day concluded that the youth team could wear the club's existing strip for the tournament and, so that all bases would be covered, he sent all six sets of the new shirts off to Kilburn Sports to have the cup final embroidery added.

In the end Spurs were informed that they could display their sponsor's logo. So how did the unbranded shirts make it all the way on to the Wembley pitch? Laundry lady Sylvie Webb clearly remembers that the day before the final, Spurs' kit man Johnny Wallis didn't know where the shirts for the match were. "He was getting very stressed," she recalls, "and it wasn't until lunchtime that he was informed that they were in Peter Day's office where they'd been sitting since coming back from the embroiderers".

Educated guesswork can now piece together what happened next. We know that Wallis only ever took two sets of shirts to a match. So, somewhat pressed for time and

*Right: Ossie Ardiles (left, shirt without sponsor) and Chris Hughton (right, shirt with sponsor) tussle with Coventry City's Cyrille Regis*

*Below: The big kit mix-up was front-page news*

slightly flustered, he almost certainly went to Day's office and, from the box of strips, selected two sets of outfield shirts numbered 2-14. With no idea that some of the shirts were sponsored and some were not, he would only have been concentrating on getting the right numbers (and ensuring he had two long-sleeved No.3 shirts for Mitchell Thomas). As was his usual routine, he would have folded each one in half, with the number facing out, before packing them away to be shipped to Wembley.

In the Wembley dressing room the following day, Wallis would have unpacked the folded kit and laid it out in his usual manner – a towel, a slip, socks, shorts and shirt resting on top with the number again facing up so that each player could identify their kit. Once the players came in after the warm-up they would have put on their shirts and then their cup final tracksuit tops on top. As Richard Gough remembers: "What's on your shirt is the last thing on your mind as you prepare to walk out for a cup final."

With all the players in their cup final tracksuit tops, as the team prepared to leave the dressing room no-one realised that half of the outfield players in the starting line-up – Gough, Gary Mabbutt, Paul Allen, Glenn Hoddle and Ossie Ardiles – plus substitute Gary Stevens did not have 'Holsten' on their shirts.

"No-one noticed," said Ardiles later, while Mabbutt recalls: "It was only after we took off our tracksuit tops and lined up for the kick-off that Chris Hughton said, 'Hey, you haven't got Holsten on your shirt.'"

The game kicked off and Bob Roberts and his delegation from Hummel UK noticed the issue immediately. Spurs chairman Irving Scholar, sitting in the Royal Box, was alerted to the problem during the first half whilst the club's new commercial manager, Mike Rollo, who was sitting with a Holsten representative, left the ground before half-time and walked round to the tunnel doors where the coaches drive in in an attempt to gain access to the dressing room and try and fix the issue. He couldn't get past the stewards and police. There is no doubt that the meticulous Wallis would also have noticed, but the fact that the problem was not fixed after half-time ("It wasn't even mentioned," insists Gough) indicates that both of the sets of shirts brought for the offending numbers must have been unsponsored.

*The Spurs team walk out for the showpiece occasion in their tracksuit tops, blissfully unaware of the mix-up*

"The second half started and nothing had changed," remembers Rollo. "I couldn't do anything and I hate to say it but, while in my heart I wanted Spurs to win, in my head I was thinking that if we triumphed Richard Gough would lift the trophy with no Holsten on his shirt and that picture would go around the world."

Immediately after the match – which Spurs lost 3-2, the first ever FA Cup final defeat for a Tottenham Hotspur team – there was a theory that the mix-up had been deliberately staged by Holsten to gain publicity, the incident making front-page news and provoking mocking from a rival beer brand, who ran an ad featuring Glenn Hoddle in a shirt without a sponsor logo under the strapline 'I bet he drinks Carling Black Label!'

Spurs were of course extremely embarrassed. Peter Day publicly described it as "a major cock-up" and added, "Holsten have registered a furious protest and who can blame them. We shall be holding a full inquiry. No one has yet discovered what went wrong. The man who is in charge of the players' kit, Johnny Wallis, has no idea how the slip-up happened."

Reeling from all the adverse publicity, Spurs quickly demanded an explanation from Hummel. "We gathered all the evidence we could to show them that it was not our mistake," remembers Roberts.

In the week following the final, emergency discussions were held between the club and Holsten – no doubt somewhat placated by the huge global publicity the mix-up had inadvertently given them – agreed that their sponsorship would continue, although in his autobiography Scholar says they were given increased advertising space at White Hart Lane in compensation.

The major casualties of the resulting fall out were Day, who departed the club after the final, and the legendary Wallis, who was put in charge of the reserves and youth team kit with Roy Reyland replacing him as head kit man.

As a postscript to the story, the shirts resurfaced for Tony Galvin's testimonial in October 1987 when the Spurs team wore a set of previously unused long-sleeved jerseys from the final, complete with the FA Cup final embroidery… and Holsten logos!

*Left: If Spurs had won the cup, skipper Richard Gough would have had to lift the cup wearing a sponsorless shirt*

*Above: Rival beer brand Carling poked fun at Holsten with this cheeky newspaper ad*

# FA CUP FINAL 1987

*Match worn by* RICHARD GOUGH

*Captain Richard Gough's shirt did not have a Holsten logo, which would have been a huge embarrassment to the club had he lifted the trophy*

*Match shirt of* CLIVE ALLEN

F.A. CUP FINAL
1987

HOLSTEN

*Clive Allen's spare long-sleeved shirt from the infamous final, complete with the beer company's logo*

# HOME 1987–89

*Match worn by* PAUL GASCOIGNE

Overshadowed by the furore over the lack of their sponsor's logos on half of the team's shirts during the 1987 FA Cup final was the fact that Spurs had previewed their new home shirt during the showpiece occasion.

The new Hummel design would again have a two-season lifespan, with navy shorts reintroduced to the ensemble following the match at Wembley. Another template design that represented a further stylistic evolution for the manufacturer, a similar style was used for several other teams' shirts including, notably, Real Madrid and the Welsh national side.

A white non-contrasting v-neck collar, which featured a single navy trim, represented another significant change. Some of the players chose to fold in the collars, giving a completely different 'collarless' appearance which has wrongly prompted some to believe that there were two versions of this design.

The traditional Hummel chevrons appeared in a subtle white shadow pattern integrated into the fabric of the shirt, creating a zig-zag background effect, as well as in the subtle, non-contrasting tape running down the sleeves (right, centre). The numbers were sublimated on the reverse.

Variations of the players' shirts during its lifetime saw the club crest appear in both embroidered and embossed versions, with the latter to be found on the replica version available for supporters to buy.

The commercial relationship with shirt sponsor Holsten survived the FA Cup final fiasco, but the design of the logo changed from the shirt's initial incarnation as per the beer brand's new look, which was unveiled in 1988.

Gascoigne, 'Gazza' to one and all, was only at Spurs for three years but the mercurial Geordie would become one of the English game's modern legends for his famous exploits in Tottenham colours and his infamous yet lovable behaviour out of them.

*Above: Gazza on the ball during the home league match against Arsenal in September 1988*

*Right: The 1987/88 jersey featured the previous version of the Holsten logo, as seen on this Clive Allen shirt, worn for the striker's final Spurs appearance*

# AWAY 1988-91

*Match worn by* CHRIS WADDLE

For the start of the 1988/89 season, Hummel reintroduced yellow – not seen for five years since the one-off centenary third shirt of 1982/83 – as a Spurs away shirt colour.

The new jersey, with its wraparound v-neck and cuffs with navy trim, featured some innovative design features – notably a bold double chevron pattern on the upper part of the sleeves and the incorporation of the manufacturer's wordmark in the fabric, the lettering being sublimated in a pattern with 'Hummel' appearing upside down on every other line.

Appearing the year before the double chevron pattern featured on the home jersey, this shirt had a three-season lifespan. However, for the second two seasons an additional pair of chevrons appeared lower down the arm on the long-sleeved variation of the shirt. From its second season of use, the shirt also included the revised cockerel crest designed by chairman Irving Scholar that also adorned that season's new home shirt.

For these final two season of the lifespan of this jersey, Spurs had no official third shirt, which was perhaps indicative of the worsening relationship between the club and Hummel. This contributed to a highly unusual situation on a misty afternoon on 19 December 1990 when the referee for Spurs' visit to Maine Road deemed Manchester City's sky blue shirts to be clashing with Tottenham's yellow ones and, following the warm-up, ordered the home side to change and play the match in their maroon away strip.

*Above: Chris Waddle in the short-sleeved variation of this shirt, despite the snowy conditions, against Sheffield Wednesday*

*Right: From 1989/90 the jersey featured the new club crest and two sets of chevrons on the long-sleeved version*

# HOME 1989–91

*Match worn by* STEVE SEDGLEY

Hummel's third and final Spurs home shirt was based on the design template of the yellow away shirt first used during the previous season with – apart from the obvious change in colour – a few subtle differences.

The simple v-neck collar with a navy blue trim was finished with a navy lozenge that featured the interlocking monogram 'THFC', echoing the style used in the ball of the club crest. The navy piping – which ran from the collar to the armpit – separated the main body and the arms, whereas the same trim went around the shoulder on the away version.

In addition, a newly revamped and coloured club crest, which in his autobiography Irving Scholar claimed he designed personally in a bid to stop trademark infringement, appeared on this shirt for the first time.

As with the away shirt, the club's 'THFC' initials and the manufacturer's name were sublimated into the man-made fabric on alternating lines. The long-sleeved versions carried two pairs of double chevrons, whereas the short-sleeved shirts only had one pair for obvious reasons. Another feature of this popular shirt design was that the numbers were of a 3D-effect block design and sublimated into the material, making it impossible to replicate and therefore easy for collectors to spot a genuine player shirt.

This was to be the last Spurs shirt produced by the much-loved Danish manufacturer as their contract with the club was to come to a very abrupt end just before the 1991 FA Cup final. Hummel did produce a full set of kit for the match, but by then the relationship between the club and the Danish parent company had become fractured beyond repair and a deal with Umbro was done in time for the Wembley showpiece against Nottingham Forest.

This very stylish shirt was extremely popular with the Spurs supporters and brings back great memories of the 1991 FA Cup run, especially Gazza's famous free-kick against Arsenal in the semi-final at Wembley.

*Above: Steve Sedgley shouts instructions against Arsenal at Highbury in August 1990*

*Right: From the start of the 1990/91 season football league badges (right) appeared on each sleeve*

# SUITED & BOOTED

Given the sizable differences between the shirts of yesteryear and their modern inheritors, it might be seen as a welcome contrast that the official tracksuits worn by Tottenham have remained broadly the same.

Dress tracksuits, walk out tops or modern day 'anthem jackets' have usually been reserved for the big occasions, notably worn for the thrilling moment the team walks on to the pitch for a cup final. They serve a functional purpose in providing comfort for the immediate pre-match routine, as well as delivering a measure of sartorial elegance before the 'reveal' of the shirt itself.

The earliest incarnations of the match specific Spurs tracksuit top come from the heyday of the 1960s. For both the 1961 and 1962 FA Cup finals Spurs wore tracksuit tops which were plain white with navy collars, cuffs and stripe down each arm, with a large navy cockerel (without surrounding shield) and detail particular to the match embroidered on the front. On the back in large capitals was stitched the simple word 'SPURS'.

For the following finals of the late 1960s and 70s the large 'SPURS' wording remained emblazoned across the back, with subtle changes to the design, the crest and the match detail. A notable anomaly, however, was the colour change to the detail and trim on the 1971 League Cup final, now in royal blue, which matched the embroidery on the match shirts and the unusually coloured shorts. These tops also, for the first time, included Umbro logos.

Throughout the 1970s Tottenham Hotspur followed the trend of having tracksuit tops for the players to wear prior the domestic games but unusually, since Spurs wore Umbro kit, these were made by adidas and featured the German company's classic three stripes on the arms. This is explained by the fact that Umbro was the distributor for adidas in the UK at the time, and the dark blue tops had individual players and staff names on the back.

As kit fashions and design evolved during the 1980s and beyond, tracksuits followed suit, but even with the later

*Left: Spurs captain Danny Blanchflower introduces the Duchess of Kent to his teammates before the 1961 FA Cup final*

*Above: A slightly different-looking cockerel crest appeared on the 1961 and 1962 tracksuit tops without the surrounding shield that featured on the match shirts*

incarnations from Puma in 2008 and Under Armour in 2015, less is still more when it comes to tracksuit design.

Genuine player worn tracksuit tops are highly collectable items because they are usually smart, good-looking garments connected to important, one-off events. They don't usually fetch the prices of match worn shirts from the same occasions but are highly desirable to the the completest collector.

Similar tracksuit tops from the 1971 (left) and 1973 (right) League Cup finals illustrate the strange foray into royal blue that occurred for the earlier occasion (below left)

Left: An adidas Spurs tracksuit from the 1970s. This apparent anomaly is explained by the fact that the club's kit suppliers at the time, Umbro, were also the distributors for adidas

*Ossie Ardiles, with his knees presumably 'all trembly', walks out for the 1981 FA Cup final*

1981 FA Cup final

1982 League Cup final

2002 League Cup final

2008 League Cup final

2015 League Cup final

# TOWARDS THE NEW MILLENNIUM
## 1991–2002

UMBRO, PONY & ADIDAS

# FA CUP FINAL 1991

*Match worn by* PAUL STEWART

Tottenham Hotspur sprang a major surprise when they walked out on to the famous Wembley turf for their ninth FA Cup final appearance wearing a completely new strip. But it wasn't just the new design that caused a stir; it was the fact that the kit was supplied by a completely new manufacturer – the club's old friend, Umbro.

By now there was nothing unusual about clubs changing kits at the end of the season, but a switch to a completely new supplier in time for a major cup final was another matter entirely. Only Southampton, West Ham and Liverpool had made such an adventurous step in the previous 15 years.

So when the team emerged from the Wembley tunnel in the smart new strip, Spurs had a very different look than when they had famously defeated Arsenal in the semi-final on the same pitch just five weeks earlier.

The design of the shirt – which carried the match detail 'FA CUP FINAL 1991' embroidered over two lines underneath the club crest – was uncomplicated, smart and stylish. However, the major talking point of the ensemble was the baggy navy shorts, which despite a modern cut conjured up images of football from a bygone age. The shorts represented a daring departure for Spurs and Umbro, setting a trend for the 1990s that other manufacturers were quick to follow.

The overall effect was a retro-inspired modern classic which came in stark contrast to the kit worn by opponents Nottingham Forest, also supplied by Umbro, which looked instantly dated alongside Tottenham's audacious new style.

Despite the loss of talisman Paul Gascoigne to injury in the first half, the Lilywhites – inspired by goal-scoring man of the match Paul Stewart – won a record eighth final, and the resulting financial boost (along with the sale of Gazza to Lazio) helped the club fend off a looming financial crisis that had been caused in part by the commercially disastrous Hummel venture.

*Above: Paul Stewart fires home the equaliser as Nottingham Forest's Stuart Pearce looks on in his outdated-looking shorts*

*Above: The baggy shorts worn by Spurs for the final were the talk of the nation and were swiftly adopted by other teams throughout the game. The kit also saw the return of navy socks for the first time in 24 years*

# HOME 1991/92

*Match worn by* GARY LINEKER

In a decade defined by bold and extravagant designs, Umbro's first Spurs shirt – the style used in the 1991 FA Cup final that became the home shirt for the next two seasons – was notably classy and elegant. In fact the new Umbro kit (without the cup final embroidery) was given its first league run-out for the last match of the 1990/91 season, a visit to Manchester United, just two days after the final.

As was the fashion of the time, the shirt had an inverted jacquard pattern which featured a raised Umbro double diamond detail integrated with the letters 'THFC', whilst the navy polo shirt-style collar with white trim had an unusual single button placket which was finished off with the initials 'THFC' at its base.

The short-sleeved version sported thick, non-contrasting cuffs with a navy half-moon-shaped blue flash with the word 'SPURS' within them in white – a design feature aimed squarely at the replica market. The long-sleeved version, only available to players, did not include this detail.

Domestically the numbers on the back carried Umbro branding. However, the previous season's FA Cup success meant that Spurs qualified for Europe for the first time in nearly a decade. The European Cup Winners' Cup shirt featured here, therefore, differs from the league version in that it lacks any Umbro branding in the numbers or Football League sleeve badges to comply with UEFA competition regulations. To compensate, the embroidered wordmark 'Umbro' and the double diamond logo on the right breast were over-stitched to make them thicker and stand out more. Unusually, Umbro did not provide white shorts so for the European Cup Winners' Cup campaign – in a break with tradition – Spurs played in blue shorts.

This shirt went on to be a huge seller for the club and remains one of the most popular Spurs shirts of all time.

*Above: Gary Lineker in action against SV Stockerau in the 1991 European Cup Winners' Cup. White shorts were not worn in Europe with this kit*

*Top: In Europe the shirt numbers were not allowed to feature Umbro branding*

*Above: A long-sleeved shirt (these were not available as replicas) showing the domestic number style*

# AWAY 1991-94 & THIRD 1994/95

*Match worn by* GARY LINEKER

This striking and enduringly popular Umbro shirt was, highly unusually, used by Spurs as an away or third shirt over the course of four seasons. As a consequence it is associated with numerous memorable matches, as well as one of Gary Lineker's finest moments at White Hart Lane.

Whilst the colour and general style were fairly traditional in nature, hailing from essentially the same template as the home shirt, the simplicity of the design was superseded by the addition of a striking and dramatically original sky blue and navy jagged chequerboard pattern across the right shoulder. Umbro's promotional material described the design as an 'ice effect'. It was certainly original and many considered it 'cool', but the pattern also became affectionately compared by some supporters to something that might be left behind by a pigeon.

Despite the tongue-in-cheek comparisons with something less than pleasant, there is no doubt that this shirt is fondly remembered by Spurs fans as it featured in numerous great moments, including Ronnie Rosenthal's four goals away at Southampton in the FA Cup in March 1995.

The actual shirt pictured here is believed to have been worn by Gary Lineker in the European Cup Winners' Cup second round first leg against Porto on 23 October 1992 at White Hart Lane. At the time, UEFA competition regulations stipulated that in the event of a colour clash the home team changed.

Tottenham defeated Porto 3-1 in the game, with Lineker scoring twice. His first was one of the all-time great Spurs team goals, with an intricate first-time passing move finished off by the No.10 from just outside the six-yard box.

*Above: Gary Lineker and Spurs take on Porto in the Cup Winners' Cup in 1992 – a rare outing for this shirt in a home match at White Hart Lane*

*Left: Following the advent of the Premier League in 1992/93 the new sleeve badges for shirts used in league matches had to be placed on a yellow patch to make them visible within the 'ice effect' pattern*

# HOME 1992/93

*Match worn by NAYIM*

The 1992/93 season dawned and the new Premier League era arrived to immense and lasting fanfare. Amidst the razzmatazz of the unveiling, however, the Tottenham Hotspur shirt remained essentially the same, albeit with a few low key but significant changes.

Following on from the Football League's lead in 1990, the new competition stipulated that its own branded sleeve badges must be worn during all league matches. The new triangular patches were applied to each sleeve and were initially made out of vinyl. However, the patches were not very robust and were easily damaged during the rigours of regular industrial washing in clubs' laundry rooms so eventually a switch was made to cloth badges.

In the final season of its two-year lifespan the home shirt also incorporated a small design change, though not for the entire season. Early in 1992 Umbro updated its company logo, with the wordmark under the double diamond becoming capitalised. But with the club using up older shirt stock the newly branded versions did not appear on the Spurs players until well into the campaign. The shirt continued to carry the heat-applied felt Umbro-branded numbers but as yet there were no players' names above them – these would not appear until the following season.

The shirt pictured here was worn by Nayim in the home game against Liverpool on 31 October 1992. The Spaniard scored the first goal, a cracking volley from the edge of the area, in a 2-0 win. Born in Ceuta, Mohammed Ali Amar (or Nayim) had joined Spurs from Barcelona in 1988. He scored a number of special goals during his Tottenham career, with his strike in the Premier League's inaugural season in this lilywhite shirt one of his finest.

Above: Nayim tussles with Chelsea's Graeme Le Saux – also sporting Umbro – at White Hart Lane in December 1992

Above: The first Premier League badges, introduced for the 1992/93 season, were made from a shiny vinyl material

# HOME 1993–95

*Match worn by* GHEORGHE POPESCU

Now mid-way through their four-year contract with Spurs, Umbro's second home shirt saw the manufacturer play it safe, especially in comparison with the classic – and certainly brave – design of its predecessor. This shirt is notable for the introduction of a third colour, as well as being the first Tottenham Hotspur shirt to include player names on the back.

The short-sleeved version of this shirt saw the addition of a yellow trim to the cuffs, making it the first post 1898 Spurs home shirt to include a colour other than white (or cream) or navy.

The long-sleeved version – in this case worn by Romanian international Gheorghe 'Gica' Popescu – was again not available as a replica and was finished with a navy cuff with white trim (but with no yellow). The sleeves were also adorned with cloth Premier League badges.

The front of both versions of the shirt carried a small Umbro stamp – 'Official Product Choice of Champions' – which harked back to the similar stamp found on the cotton shirts of the late 1960s and early 1970s. It also featured an unusual two-tier navy collar with a two-lined white trim. The Umbro double diamond was sublimated into the fabric and, as was found on many of the Umbro designs at the time, the Spurs club crest was applied within a retro, oversized shield.

Probably the most fundamental change to the shirt that appeared at this time was the introduction of players' names to the back. Names had appeared on the backs of shirts in the past – memorably in the North American Soccer League of the mid-to-late 1970s, and then an international precedent was set by Scotland in 1979. But the second season of the Premier League saw the idea adopted permanently and the players ran out with their names printed above their squad numbers from the start of the 1993/94 season – the concept having been trialled in the domestic cup finals of 1993. This, of course, spawned a lucrative additional dimension to the replica kit market.

*Above: Gica Popescu on the ball*

*Right: Cloth Premier League sleeve badges were introduced for the 1993/94 season*

*Top: Player names were spelt out in heat-applied navy flock letters. The numbers were cloth stitch-applied and included the Umbro logo and wordmark at the base of each numeral*

*Above: A short-sleeved example, worn by Nicky Barmby*

# THIRD 1991–94

*Match shirt of* DARREN ANDERTON

As part of a growing trend during the 1990s, Umbro released this third shirt in 1991, although its first competitive outing did not come until the European Cup Winners' Cup clash with Feyenoord at White Hart Lane in March 1992.

The design had its origins in the template for a goalkeeper's jersey called the 'Euro', which was available via the manufacturer's 'Teamwear' catalogue from which amateur teams could kit themselves out. This design had the letters 'UMBRO' across the upper body of the shirt in a varying pinstripe pattern that gave each letter a fade effect. For Tottenham's sky blue third shirt the lettering 'SPURS' appeared on both the front and back (and also wrapped around the left leg of the shorts). Umbro made similar bespoke shirts for both Ajax and Inter Milan.

The collar was navy blue with a light blue trim, and popper buttons held the collar down at the front. A single-button placket repeated the pinstripe pattern of the upper half of the shirt, while Umbro's double diamond on the right breast was now picked out in navy and in-filled in white.

The THFC/Umbro tonal combination within the fabric was featured on the bottom half of the jersey, which also included twin navy vertical pinstripes. Each sleeve included Premier League badges, but the pattern on this particular shirt made them hard to see. To compensate, recycled vinyl badges from the 1992/93 season were heat-applied to a sky blue-coloured patch and stitched on to each sleeve. The letters and numbers were in flock material, and the numbers used a 3D-effect font and included the manufacturer's logo at the bottom of each numeral.

The Darren Anderton shirt pictured here was prepared for the 1993/94 season but never used as new Premier League regulations stipulated that the letters of the name must include a border to make them stand out.

This shirt was only worn six times across the three seasons in which it saw competitive use.

*Above: Darren Anderton on one of the rare occasions when this third shirt saw action*

*Right: A David Howells shirt showing the lettering style that was later adopted. This shirt was worn against Newcastle in the opening game of the 1993/94 season*

*Above: The Premier League sleeve badges were placed on a patch to make them stand out*

# AWAY 1994/95

*Match worn by* JURGEN KLINSMANN

One of the most famous Spurs shirts of the modern era, the jersey featured here is the actual shirt worn by Jurgen Klinsmann when he performed his famous 'dive' celebration against Sheffield Wednesday.

The popular navy design, with purple abstract patterns on the right side and left sleeve, was the last Umbro shirt produced for the club and the last to display the Holsten logo (for the time being at least). In keeping with Umbro's generic designs of the period, the club crest was incorporated into a shield, although oddly this was a different shape to the one that appeared on the club's home shirt.

The shirt was unveiled around the time that Spurs made an adventurous summer foray into the transfer market, with the capture of the German World Cup winner the standout piece of business. But with Klinsmann came a reputation for theatrical diving, which became a talking point in the run-up to the 1994/95 season.

During Klinsmann's first match away to Sheffield Wednesday, having been mocked and jeered by the home fans throughout the game, the German striker silenced the boos in the 82nd minute with Spurs' fourth and decisive goal in a 4-3 thriller. He then launched into an exaggerated dive celebration alongside his teammates, endearing himself to Spurs fans and the watching world by mocking his reputation. It is one of the club's iconic Premier League moments and set the tone for Klinsmann's eventful Tottenham career.

Worn just five more times after that, this was nevertheless a popular away shirt, although its dark colour meant it was not suitable for cup competitions as it clashed with the black of the officials. For this reason the yellow away kit first worn in 1991/92 needed to be retained as a 'third' choice for cup matches.

*Jurgen Klinsmann launches into his iconic 'dive' celebration. Because of the huge demand for shirts with 'Klinsmann' on the back following the German's sensational debut, the Spurs club shop ran out of the letter N*

# HOME 1995–97

*Match worn by* GARY MABBUTT

The summer of 1995 saw Spurs sign with another new kit supplier after Umbro's four-year contract came to an end. The club turned to American sportswear and street apparel brand Pony, signalling not only a change in kit manufacturer but also a (temporary) end to Spurs' association with sponsors Holsten, who were replaced by computer company Hewlett-Packard.

Pony was founded in Canada in the early 1970s by Dutch-born ex-goalkeeper Emile Salamon. In 1972, flamboyant Uruguayan businessman Roberto Muller brought the company to the USA, financed by Andre Guelfi and Horst Dassler, and the company provided the great Pele with his boots for a time during his spell in the North American Soccer League and was a big name in other high-profile American sports. It wasn't until 2001 that the letters were marketed as standing for 'Product Of New York'.

The company's association with Spurs was preceded by deals with other Premier League clubs such as West Ham, Coventry and Southampton, although the tie-up with Tottenham was certainly its most prestigious contract.

Without the same brand recognition in football enjoyed by the likes of its predecessor, Umbro, Pony faced an uphill battle to win over the doubters. At first glance, Pony's debut home jersey bore a resemblance to the style of the 1991 shirt, but that is where the similarities ended.

The capitalised Pony wordmark appeared on the right breast. On the crest, the lions and motto scroll were removed leaving the cockerel perched on top of a ball and monogram, which were encompassed within a rather odd-looking triangular shield. The crest, a shadow of which also featured in the jacquard pattern, echoed designs from the 1950s. The '*Audere est Facere*' text that had appeared below the crest was changed to a gothic font and moved to the base of an unusual, heavy-looking placket, which had three large buttons that broadened out to a navy polo collar with white trim.

*Above: Gary Mabbutt sports the first Pony Spurs kit against Newcastle*

*Top right: Manufacturer's branding within the numerals was banned from the 1995/96 campaign*

*Right: Initially Pony's chevron taping featured on the sleeves of all the players' shirts. However, by October 1995 it had disappeared from the long-sleeved version (right)*

# AWAY 1995/96 & THIRD 1996/97

*Match worn by* CHRIS ARMSTRONG

In the four years of its contract with Spurs, Pony certainly came up with some outlandish designs. For this shirt the manufacturer continued the popular navy and purple colour scheme used by Umbro in the previous away shirt, although without the same success.

The navy-and-purple-striped shirt replicated many of the details of its home counterpart, including the club crest on the unusually shaped white shield outlined in navy and the Pony capitalised wordmark logo. It continued to feature the company's own font for the letters and numbers, which were also carried on the home shirt. There were, however, some key differences. It featured just two buttons in a straight and rather more standard placket, and had a navy collar that, just like the home shirt, faded after a number of washes and ran into what was originally a white trim. The club's motto did not appear anywhere on the shirt.

This style was registered and advertised as the away shirt for the 1995/96 season but, in a similar fashion to the previous season's Umbro away kit, it necessitated the introduction of a lighter yellow third jersey. This was because its dark colour had the potential to clash with the uniforms of the match officials, who still wore black in domestic cup competition.

It became the designated third shirt for the 1996/97 season but was never worn in a competitive game during that campaign.

*Chris Armstrong (left) celebrates with Darren Anderton (right) and goalscorer Teddy Sheringham during a rare outing for this shirt at Sheffield Wednesday in September 1995*

# THIRD 1995/96, AWAY 96/97 & THIRD 97/98

*Match worn by* COLIN CALDERWOOD

Pony's third shirt for the 1995/96 season swapped duties with its navy and purple predecessor to become the away shirt for the following season, and then reverted back to being the third jersey in 1997/98. Initially produced as an away cup shirt – primarily due to the fact that the navy and purple strip clashed with the black worn by match officials – it proved to be one of the American company's more popular designs.

This shirt was worn in cup competitions against Hereford United, Chester and Coventry in the 1995/96 season as well as in the final two league games of the campaign against Leeds and Newcastle. However, it saw most of its service as the 1996/97 away shirt.

The combination of a yellow shirt teamed with yellow shorts and socks, with navy detailing, was very much in line with the classic Spurs away kit tradition. However, in a clear break with previous incarnations, for the first time the shirt sported contrasting sleeves in navy.

The crest and the word 'SPURS' were sublimated into the fabric of the main body and sleeves in a complex tonal pattern, with the logos of the manufacturer and the club's Hewlett-Packard sponsor in navy. The stylish polo shirt collar once again differed from contemporary alternatives, with a navy 'V' insert and yellow trim. The cuffs reversed the rest of the shirt's colour styling, with the trim this time picked out in dark blue.

Although the shirt nominally reverted back to use as a third kit for the 1997/98 season, it was not used that season. However, sets were prepared with the new universal Premier League letters and numbers as seen on the back of the David Ginola No.14 shirt *(right)*.

*Above: Colin Calderwood in action against Derby in 1997. The shirt pictured here (right) was worn by Calderwood during the 7-1 defeat to Newcastle in December 1996*

*Left: A shirt prepared for David Ginola for the 1997/98 season with the new Premier League letters and numbers*

# HOME 1997–99

*Match worn by* LES FERDINAND

Considered by many to be Pony's best Spurs offering, this plain white shirt with navy embellishments was simplistic and very much designed in the traditional Tottenham Hotspur style.

Central to that was the variation on the club crest that was used, which was more a coat of arms than a badge and was possibly introduced in response to criticism of the design which appeared on the first Pony shirts. This style of Tottenham crest was not new, it originated from the 1950s when it had been prepared in readiness for the club's 75th anniversary with legendary 1951 title-winning manager Arthur Rowe said to have been involved in its original design. It was used on a number of club publications over the years but had never appeared on a Spurs shirt until now. The design featured multiple symbols and meanings that represented local landmarks in recognition of the roots and heritage of the club. In addition, on the 1997/98 home shirt the latin motto *'Audere est Facere'* appeared on the back in a navy gothic font.

The collar of the previous home shirt was replaced with a stylish navy wrapover v-neck with double white stripes, with this styling repeated in the cuffs. Twin navy piping ran down the v-neck to the cuffs, and the tonal fabric featured a ribbed stripe pattern. However, the material proved uncomfortable for the players and a perceived lack of quality was consistently the biggest criticism of Pony's Tottenham products over the years.

This season also saw the introduction of a universal font for letters and numbers across the Premier League, with the league's logos also appearing in the base of each numeral. Chris Kay International won the license to provide Premier League clubs with the larger player letters, numbers and branded sleeve badges in a trademarked felt material called 'Lextra'.

*Left: Les Ferdinand in action for Spurs against Manchester United in August 1998 during Pony's final season as the club's kit supplier*

*Above: The 1997/98 season saw the use of a 'coat of arms' club crest first used in the 1950s*

# AWAY 1997/98

*Match shirt of* JURGEN KLINSMANN

The pace of development in football jersey design and manufacture was rapidly gaining speed by the late '90s as the success of the Premier League saw a huge increase in the commercial operations of its clubs.

When this stylish shirt was unveiled there was some surprise at the colour scheme: a combination of navy blue and a colour new to most fans, described as 'ecru' – a light beige that mimics the tone of unbleached linen – which entered the football kit lexicon when it was used in a range of team strips during this era.

The shirt, used for only one season, utilised the same wrapover v-neck collar and cuff design as the home shirt and a third colour – gold – was also used for the crest surround, the sponsor and manufacturer's logos, the sleeve panel trims, and the letters and numbers on the back. There was contrasting navy and gold trim for the cuffs and the ecru colour extended to the under-arm panels.

This Jurgen Klinsmann shirt was prepared for use during his 'second coming' as a Tottenham player. When Klinsmann had exercised his right to leave at the end of the 1994/95 season it had prompted an outburst from chairman Alan Sugar that he "would not wash my car" with the German's shirt. But almost three years later the pair made up, and Klinsmann's nine goals in a five-month loan spell played a major part in the club staving off relegation.

*Above: Jurgen Klinsmann's return coincided with the introduction of a new colour into the Spurs palette – ecru*

*Above: For the 1997/98 season the Premier League sleeve patches included a small 'TM' symbol above the end of the lion's tail*

# AWAY 1998/99

*Match shirt of* DAVID GINOLA

The purple seen on Pony's first away shirt of 1995/96 was reintroduced on this jersey – one of the American manufacturer's more popular Spurs shirts – and again it was only used for a single season. The shirt gave Spurs a look reminiscent of the classic viola colours of Fiorentina, injecting a dash of continental style and swagger.

The main theme of this minimalist, uncluttered shirt – which was first worn away to Southampton – was the vibrant colour. The non-contrasting wrapover v-neck collar had a white trim, whilst the white piping stood out from the purple hue and ran down from the neck to each armpit.

This jersey continued the use of the 1950s coat of arms crest seen on the home and previous season's away shirts. Against the plain, silky-looking purple body of the shirt, in a ribbed material similar to the home shirt, the crest detailing was set against a navy background. In fact, the crest is the only place on the shirt where any colours other than purple and white were used.

The style and flair of this shirt's design were exemplified in the player who wore this particular example, David Ginola. Signed in 1997, the French winger added some much-needed elan and glamour to a side struggling to make a meaningful impression, particularly in the league. For all his showbiz looks and appeal, Ginola was also a highly effective attacking player who swiftly became the darling of the White Hart Lane crowd. It was his name that many fans wanted on their replica shirts during his stint at the club.

The players' match shirts in the Pony era had no additional performance technology compared to their replica equivalents. As with a number of the smaller manufacturers at the time, the shirts the players wore were exactly the same as those that Spurs supporters could buy in the shop.

*David Ginola – pictured here in a pre-season friendly – looked good in any colour... even bright purple*

# LEAGUE CUP FINAL 1999

*Match worn by* DAVID GINOLA

For all the struggles and occasional false dawns of Spurs during the 1990s – punctuated by a rapid turnover of six managers in eight years – a trophy was secured at the end of the decade thanks to a third League Cup win, this time over Leicester City. It had been eight seasons since a Spurs kit supplier had needed to produce a set of shirts for a showpiece final and Pony marked the occasion with this variation on the home jersey.

Pony's final Tottenham shirt included the usual match detail embroidery and – for the first time on a Spurs shirt – the competition sponsor's sleeve badges. Arced over the top of the club crest was embroidered the text 'WORTHINGTON CUP FINAL', with 'WEMBLEY 1999' below, all in navy. Bass Breweries, for whom Worthington was a brand of beer, had taken over the sponsorship of the League Cup competition that season and their final-specific felt patches were heat-applied on to each sleeve. It was the first time Spurs wore anything other than league badges on their sleeves, but they still carried the standard Premier League names and numbers on the back.

Spurs were led out on to the Wembley pitch by manager George Graham. For the final he wore a club blazer not featuring the crest his players sported but the previous plain cockerel-and-ball design. Graham, the former Arsenal favourite whose controversial appointment in October 1998 had been greeted with disquiet by large sections of the Tottenham fanbase, earned a reprieve thanks to winning the final, despite Spurs going down to 10 men following Justin Edinburgh's dismissal after an hour. They secured the trophy with a last-minute Allan Nielsen header.

It was perhaps not David Ginola's most memorable display in Spurs colours, but it marked his only honour in English football.

*David Ginola on the ball during the 1999 Worthington Cup final, when new competition-specific felt sleeve patches were worn (above)*

# HOME 1999–2001

*Match worn by* STEFFEN IVERSEN

The last year of the millennium brought a mixture of something old and something very new to the Spurs shirt. The latter was Tottenham's first kit deal with one of the global industry leaders in adidas, whilst there was a clear nod to the recent past with the return of Holsten to the front of the new shirts.

The partnership with the famous brand was a breath of fresh air for everyone at Spurs – staff, players and supporters alike. The first adidas home kit was actually unveiled in the last home game of 1998/99 season against Chelsea, with the range formally launched on 15 July 1999.

The popularity of the adidas shirts compared to their Pony predecessors was reflected in increased sales in the brand-new megastore at White Hart Lane, with chairman Alan Sugar later stating in the company accounts that sales had "bucked the negative trend reported by other clubs".

However, in hindsight this era is considered a relative low point in the history of adidas football shirt design. The period saw a general shift in the emphasis of kit designers from the extravagent, consumer-led designs of the 1990s to an increased focus on assisting performance. In a response to the so-called 'base layer' technology being pioneered by Under Armour, who were formed in the USA in 1996, and the forward-thinking designs of brands like Kappa, adidas developed their 'Climalite' performance fabric designed to make the shirts significantly lighter and more comfortable for the players. Perhaps as a result of this shift in emphasis, the shirt designs themselves were somewhat unadventurous and unimaginative in comparison to their recent predecessors.

The new home shirt itself went back to the always popular basics of plain white with navy trim, featuring a large navy collar with a v-insert. On the left breast was a modern take on the 1983 incarnation of the crest and opposite was the adidas 'Equipment' logo (which had come to replace the iconic 'old skool' trefoil logo in the early part of the decade).

*Above: Steffen Iversen wears the long-sleeved version of Spurs' first-ever adidas shirt against Coventry at White Hart Lane*

*Right: The shirt featured navy piping either side of the three adidas stripes on the shoulders, with the cuff design significantly different on the short-sleeved version*

# AWAY 1999/2000

*Match worn by* ALLAN NIELSEN

Manufacturers adidas gave the traditional Spurs away colours of yellow and navy a twist for their first alternative offering for the club. The shirt divided opinion and the team experienced mixed fortunes whilst wearing it – including a 6-1 defeat in the FA Cup at Newcastle.

The relatively complex construction of the shirt, with the navy sleeve colour running across the shoulders, was from an adidas template rolled out across several clubs and – when paired with white shorts and white and navy socks – did not look particularly 'Spurs' to some.

The shirt was mainly a mustard yellow, with the cut of the contrasting navy sleeves giving the main body a bib-like appearance. The two primary colours were separated by white piping.

The three white adidas stripes extended all the way down to navy cuffs, which were trimmed with white, and the white collar was a similar design to that seen on the home shirt but without the v-insert. The names and numbers on the back were in navy. There was a yellow adidas 'Equipment' tag stitched into the seam on the left side of the shirt, near the hip, which only appears on the player shirts.

The Stephen Carr shirt *(bottom right)* differs from the Premier League version worn by Allan Nielsen *(far right)*. It was prepared for use in the UEFA Cup but never worn as an early exit to Kaiserslautern in the second round meant that the shirts were left hanging and unused in the kit room. This version differed from those worn in the Premier League in that there were no logos in the base of the numbers and they did not carry sleeve badges.

*Above: Allan Nielsen, with his sleeves rolled up and sporting navy shorts to avoid a colour clash, in a tangle away at Leeds*

*Right: A shirt with unbranded Premier League numbers that was prepared for use in the UEFA Cup but never worn*

# AWAY 2000/01

*Match worn by* LEDLEY KING

The third adidas design for Tottenham pleased traditionalists with its mainly plain navy, 1960s-inspired palette. It was the first full navy Spurs shirt since the Hummel days but was regarded as unimaginative by a small minority who felt that adidas had played it safe.

Premier League match officials usually now wore green which meant that such a dark colour could be safely adopted, but this shirt still only had five competitive outings, including a 4-3 loss at Leeds and defeats at Derby, Southampton and Coventry. Not remembered as a 'lucky' shirt, then, the only time it didn't taste defeat was when it was worn in a 0-0 draw at Brentford.

One of the last in the trend for 'baggy' shirts which was the fashion during the 1990s, the main body of the jersey was trimmed in white throughout. The non-contrasting navy collar was a smart combination of a wrapover v-neck with a broad white trim. An eye-catching detail was the addition of a white label on the back of the collar that was inscribed with the word 'SPURS'.

The famous adidas three stripes ran down the full length of each sleeve, but on the short-sleeved version the two outer stripes splayed out to form the cuff. On the long-sleeved version the stripes ran the complete length of the sleeve and stopped at a plain navy cuff.

Incorporated into each side of the shirt from the armpit to the midpoint of the jersey – and dividing the front and back – was a silky white mesh panel. The shirt was stylishly finished at the bottom with a broad white trim which formed the hem.

The appeal of this particular shirt lies not only with the design but also because it was worn by long-serving defender Ledley King, who remembers it as one of his favourites.

*Above: On the short-sleeved version of this shirt the outer two of the three adidas stripes splayed out to form the cuffs*

*Left: Ledley King in action against Derby. Despite a chronic knee condition that restricted much of his later career, King is widely regarded as one of the club's greatest-ever defenders*

# HOME 2001/02

*Match worn by* DEAN RICHARDS

The last adidas Spurs home shirt, produced for the final year of the German manufacturer's three-year contract, was unveiled amidst a growing mood of optimism at the club following the return of Glenn Hoddle as manager in March 2001.

However, like the 1999–2001 home jersey, the design itself is representative of what is thought by some fans to be a somewhat uninspired time for adidas football shirt design. This shirt, then, very much represented evolution rather than revolution.

One interesting development was the increase in shirt technology around this time, with advanced fabrics and features being incorporated into the player jerseys to increase comfort and, in theory, improve performance.

The 2001/02 home shirt was made from adidas's technologically advanced 'Climalite' material which had a wicking effect designed to absorb the sweat from the body and allow it to evaporate. The navy three-quarter panels down the side of the shirt and under the sleeves were made of a mesh material to provide ventilation. Inside the shirt itself the backs of the embroidered club crest and adidas logo were covered with a hyper-fixed material, commonly called 'webbing', to reduce irritation to the players' skin. The sharp v-neck collar was also much sturdier than on the replica versions, designed to withstand the rigours of top-flight football. This was the first Spurs shirt, then, that differed greatly in its construction to its replica version.

Tragically, the incumbent of the jersey pictured, Dean Richards, died at the age of 36 in 2011 having been forced to retire on medical advice six years earlier. Richards had joined from Southampton for £8.1 million in 2001 and made 73 league appearances in four seasons at White Hart Lane.

*Dean Richards points the way forward during the FA Cup third round match against Coventry City in January 2002. A rugged centre-half, Richards' Spurs career was sadly dogged by health and fitness issues*

# AWAY 2001/02

*Match worn by* GUS POYET

The third and final season of adidas's stint as Tottenham's kit supplier saw another change of away shirt, meaning that for each of their three seasons the German manufacturer had produced a new away shirt that was only used for a single campaign.

As its primary colour the shirt adopted possibly the lightest shade of blue that Spurs had worn since the reversed-halves home shirt of the 1880s or perhaps the alternative change jersey which was worn just once during the early 1930s. While other light blue designs had since been worn, chiefly during the mid-1980s, this shirt represented a significant alteration, with its more understated pastel tone contrasting with the almost neon blues of nearly 20 years previously.

In terms of style, detail and features, this shirt was almost an exact reverse of the home shirt, including the standout navy panels under the arms. The v-neck was in navy and edged by a narrower white trim, although the cuffs lacked any such adornment and were finished in plain navy. In an unusual variation of the traditional adidas three stripes design, at the top of the shoulder the two outer stripes separated and curved away from the central stripe and splayed out as they reached the neck. In contrast to the club's previous light blue shirts, this version was often paired with white shorts, which was another departure from tradition.

The style was worn against Tranmere and Fulham in Tottenham's run to the Worthington Cup final, and this particular shirt was worn by Gus Poyet – albeit combined with the more recognisable navy shorts – when he scored the winner in the away win at Leeds United as Glenn Hoddle's side looked to be making substantial progress in the manager's first full season in the job.

*The 2001/02 away shirt was a similar light blue to that worn by the Uruguay national team, which obviously suited Gus Poyet down to the ground*

# LEAGUE CUP FINAL 2002

*Match worn by* TEDDY SHERINGHAM

This is one of the more intriguing Tottenham Hotspur shirts of the modern era, and has something of a Holy Grail status amongst Spurs collectors because it is a one-off shirt produced for a special occasion due to a highly unusual set of circumstances.

After reaching the 2002 League Cup final, Spurs lost the coin toss to decide which team would have choice of colours and Blackburn Rovers selected their traditional white-and-blue-halved shirts. Unfortunately, this kit clashed with both Tottenham's home and away kits, causing a huge problem for kit supplier adidas whose deal to supply the club was due to finish at the end of the season. It meant that adidas had to produce a whole new strip for the final that they were unable, or unwilling, to mass produce and sell commercially.

In the event, the kit manufacturer produced an emergency set of approximately 60 of these yellow and blue shirts for the game at great expense, but it was never made available to buy as a replica. Consequently it is now one of the most sought after of all modern-day Spurs match shirts.

The body of the shirt was made from a yellow patterned tonal fabric, with long contrasting raglan navy sleeves (with the adidas three stripes in white) that extended over the shoulders to the neck, and a navy v-neck with white trim. The League Cup competition was still sponsored by Worthington at the time and the shirt carried the beer brand's logo on competition-specific sleeve badges. The shirt also had 'WORTHINGTON CUP FINAL CARDIFF 2002' embroidered below the club crest.

During this period domestic finals were played at the Millennium Stadium in Cardiff rather than at Wembley, which was being rebuilt, and with the arena's roof closed it was Britain's first major 'indoor' football match. Unfamiliar surroundings, then, and it showed in the performance as Spurs succumbed to a disappointing 2-1 defeat.

*Left: Teddy Sheringham takes a tumble in the one-off Spurs shirt produced for the 2002 Worthington Cup final against Blackburn Rovers*

*Above: This match worn shirt is paired with the captain's armband it was accompanied with during the final*

adidas

WORTHINGTON CUP FINAL
CARDIFF 2002

HOLSTEN

CAPTAIN

# LEAGUE CUP FINAL 2002

*Presentation shirt of* DARREN ANDERTON

The existence of this extremely rare shirt will come as a complete surprise to the majority of Spurs fans. It is a one-off home shirt prepared for the trophy presentation in the event that Tottenham had won the 2002 League Cup final.

Because of the unusual circumstances that meant the yellow and blue adidas shirt worn in the final was not going to be available to supporters – even though demand was likely to be huge should Spurs have secured a famous victory and pictures of the club's jubilant celebrations been beamed around the world – the decision was made to produce a complete set of game-specific branded home shirts. Had Spurs beaten Graeme Souness' Blackburn Rovers side, the players would have changed into these shirts for the trophy lift .

The shirts that were prepared were standard white replica home shirts, customised for the final with the requisite logos and match details for the trophy presentation. The Premier League letters and numbers were replica-sized, not the larger 'player size', and the match detail was applied with shop-sold, heat-applied felt print rather than being embroidered.

The full set of shirts was then bagged up and taken to Cardiff for the final. Kit man Roy Reyland took them into the dugout, but after Blackburn won the match the bag remained unopened and the jerseys sadly never saw the light of day.

Until now very few people were aware that shirts like this one – which would have been worn by Darren Anderton in the event of a Tottenham victory – ever existed. Even fewer had ever seen one, making them highly sought after by collectors.

*The Spurs players and staff can only look on dejectedly as Blackburn lift the 2002 Worthington Cup trophy – there was unfortunately no need for Darren Anderton or his teammates to don their special presentation shirts*

# IN SAFE HANDS

'Goalkeepers are different' is one of football's most enduring maxims, and one that is certainly reflected in the history of the kit that the custodians of the Tottenham Hotspur net have worn over the years. It is a story that starts from modest beginnings but ends with a dramatic mix of designs and a dazzling arrays of colours.

Goalkeepers were first mentioned in the rules of the game in 1871, over a decade before Hotspur FC were formed. In the game's infancy, they wore the same colours as their teammates and were distinguished from them only by wearing caps.

Then in 1909 a change in the rules required them to wear colours that significantly differed from their outfield teammates. The new regulation stipulated that only three colours were allowed – royal blue, red or white, with green added as a fourth option in 1912. Green quickly became the regular choice at Spurs – as well as most other clubs – because it was easily distinguishable and rarely clashed with opposition colours (although red would be worn in the event of a clash). In 1921 yellow was recognised by the International Football Association Board as the goalkeeper's shirt colour for internationals, and it would

be nearly 65 years before the Football League allowed goalkeepers to wear yellow in domestic club matches.

In the early years of football, a goalkeeper's jersey was literally just that – a woolen jersey, sweater or heavy roll-neck jumper. These jerseys, used until the late 1950s, would soak up water, mud and sweat and hang heavy around the wearer's shoulders.

The cockerel crest was first placed on a Spurs goalkeeper's jersey for the 1921 FA Cup final, when it was positioned centrally on the chest. Then from 1956 onwards it has always appeared in the more traditional position on the left breast.

Like most clubs, Spurs continued to stick with green as the primary goalkeeper's shirt colour through the 1960s, although blue and red were also prepared for use. In the early 1970s manufacturers' logos started to appear on the shirts, and at Spurs it was the keepers' jerseys that first sported the Umbro double diamond.

Then, when the rules over goalkeepers' shirts having to be plain and all one colour were relaxed during the 1980s, Hummel produced a wide variety of more adventurous designs. Umbro took up the baton in the early 1990s and

*Right: Pat Jennings leaps on to the back of fellow Spurs keeper Ken Hancock during a photoshoot before the 1969/70 campaign*

*Below, left: A picture of legendary Tottenham Hotspur keeper Ted Ditchburn apparently wearing an unusual red goalkeeper's jersey, although this is actually a black and white photograph that has been colourised*

*Below, centre: For the first 100 years of the club's history the primary colour for Spurs goalkeepers' shirts was green, although blue (as worn here by 1961 Double-winner Bill Brown) and red were also prepared for use*

*Far right: Barry Daines is pictured in an Admiral goalkeeper's jersey in January 1979 which, unlike the outfield shirt, remained plain and simple due to the strict Football League regulations. The white collar is actually from an outfield shirt worn underneath*

unleashed an explosion of weird and wonderful styles brought on by the advent of the Premier League in 1992 when the match officials started wearing green rather than the traditional black.

Over the years the position of goalkeeper at White Hart Lane has always been a treasured one and the incumbent has invariably had a unique bond with the club's fans. Spurs have had a number of truly world-class keepers between their sticks, but some of the former No.1s who perhaps fit more neatly into the category of terrace favourites or cult heroes retain an equal place in the supporters' affections. A leaf through the following pages of shirts – from the classic styling of the traditional jerseys to the crazed patterns of the 1990s – will bring the memory of many of these celebrated custodians back to life.

# FA CUP FINAL 1961 & 1962

*Match worn by* BILL BROWN

The two goalkeeper's jerseys featured on these pages are amongst the rarest and most historic Tottenham Hotspur shirts of them all. Both belonging to Double-winning hero Bill Brown, they were match worn during the back-to-back FA Cup triumphs of 1961 and 1962 which were at the heart of the club's glory glory years.

The 1961 jersey *(right)*, however, is actually an undershirt that was worn beneath Brown's main jersey for the final that saw Bill Nick's men famously claim the Double. This jersey was originally prepared as the match shirt, with the blue embroidery exactly as it appeared on the outfield players' white shirts, but the blue was considered too dark against the green and didn't stand out well enough. Therefore a second jersey was prepared with the club crest and match embroidery stitched on to a woolen patch that was then sewn on to a green jersey *(below, right)*.

The fabulous 1962 jersey *(far right)* was Brown's main match jersey for the 1962 FA Cup final against Burnley. This time the club crest and match detail were embroidered directly through the shirt in white so that they were clearly and easily readable.

Both of these pieces of historic Spurs memorabilia originate from the personal collection of Bill Brown, and in 2017 the 1962 jersey became the most expensive Spurs match worn shirt ever sold at auction when it hammered at £12,000. Of course, out of a set of 11 match worn shirts there is only ever one goalkeeper's jersey which explains the high price.

Like the outfield players' shirts of the era, both of these jerseys were made by Umbro and – as was the custom at the time – neither of them carried a number on the back. Everyone knew who the goalkeeper was.

*Above: The 'Choice of Champions' collar label from Bill Brown's 1962 FA Cup final jersey*

*Right: With its club crest and embroidery on a white patch, the difference between Bill Brown's match shirt and undershirt (below left) is clear*

# UMBRO 1960s

*Match worn by* PAT JENNINGS

When Pat Jennings was the primary custodian of the Spurs goal in the mid 1960s, the Tottenham Hotspur goalkeeper's jersey – like its classic lilywhite and blue outfield home counterpart – was plain, simple and stylish.

The new style cockerel-on-ball club crest was introduced in 1967 with blue embroidery, but by 1968 this had changed to white (although blue crest versions were worn up until 1971). This makes the jersey featured here extremely rare.

As was now the tradition, the Spurs goalkeeper would usually wear green, although blue (with a white crest) was sometimes used as an alternative. Pat Jennings also wore an unusual amber jersey in the UEFA Cup away match at Nantes, who wore green, in October 1971.

By 1971/72 Umbro had introduced goalkeepers' jerseys with v-insert collars, and Pat Jennings wore a royal blue version of this style for the 1973 League Cup final against Norwich City. This jersey was notable for being the first Spurs jersey to carry a prominent manufacturer's logo for a major final, with Umbro's double diamond badge being placed on the right breast. This was not present on the outfield players' shirts. And during the 1974/75 season the number '1' finally started to appear on goalkeepers' shirts.

Other than these minor changes, the Spurs goalkeeper's shirt remained virtually unchanged for the rest of the 1970s. Even when Admiral arrived and revolutionised the outfield players' shirts with their oversized collars and heavily branded piping, because goalkeepers' shirts were governed by strict football league rules that stated that the shirts must be plain and still selected from the standard four colours, goalkeepers' shirts were not immediately carried along on the wave of change. The Admiral Spurs jersey was always green and there were three different collar designs including a roll-neck. A blue version was match-prepared but never worn.

*Above: Pat Jennings played nearly 500 times for Spurs and even scored a goal in the 1967 FA Charity Shield*

*Right: Goalkeepers' shirts did not generally have the No.1 on the back until the 1974/75 season*

# LE COQ SPORTIF 1980s

*Match worn by* RAY CLEMENCE

When Le Coq Sportif took over from Admiral in 1980, they were still governed by the league regulations that stipulated that all goalkeepers' shirts had to be plain, simple and all one colour.

Green was still the club's first choice, but a blue alternative was also regularly worn. More controversially, Le Coq Sportif produced a red version which appeared on Milija Aleksic in the team photo for the 1980/81 season. But the colour was only worn on a handful of occasions, firstly in the league against West Bromwich Albion during the 1981/82 campaign and for the last time against Udinese on the Australian tour of 1985 (below, right).

Whilst the first generation of Le Coq Sportif home shirts featured a central club crest and two manufacturer's logos on the sleeves, the goalkeeper's shirts always had the crest in the traditional position on the left breast and a single manufacturer's logo on the right side, with none on the sleeves.

Like the home shirts, however, the material was made from a modern and dynamic nylon and acetate mix, and for the club's 1982/83 centenary season the goalkeeper's jerseys incorporated the stylish and revolutionary shadow stripes also found on the outfield player shirts.

Very much associated with the brilliant Ray Clemence, the Le Coq Sportif period saw a range of traditional but subtly stylish goalkeeper's jerseys. But it was very much the calm before the storm…

*Above: Although Ray Clemence generally wore a green jersey, there is something undeniably special about this blue version with the shadow stripes worn during the 1982/83 centenary season*

*Right: The green and red versions from the Le Coq Sportif Spurs goalkeeper's shirt range*

# UEFA CUP FINAL 1984

*Match worn by* TONY PARKS

Although Ray Clemence was the first choice Tottenham Hotspur goalkeeper for most of the Le Coq Sportif era, young home-grown keeper Tony Parks experienced his best-ever season in 1983/84 which coincided with the fabulous run to the final of the UEFA Cup.

Having risen through the ranks at the club since the age of 12, Parks was steeped in the history and tradition of Spurs. "It was all about that shirt," he recalls. "It was the badge. As an apprentice you helped pack the first team kit, you had to lay it out in the dressing room. You'd see that badge and that was your dream."

There is no doubt that Parks, who made his debut during the centenary season of 1982/83 and played 28 games the following season, had lilywhite and blue blood coursing through his veins. When he entered the dressing room for the first leg of the 1984 UEFA Cup final away to Anderlecht, he immediately noticed that a red goalkeeper's shirt had been laid out for him. He refused to wear it.

"I couldn't work out why red was introduced for such an occasion. I didn't think it was right that a Tottenham player should be wearing a red shirt and I made my point," he explains. "Johnny Wallis was great about it. He was the kind of kit man who would do anything to get a player out onto the pitch happy and in the right frame of mind."

A green jersey was subsequently found, and green was also worn for the second leg back at White Hart Lane. This match of course went on to be Parks' finest hour, the young keeper famously saving two penalties in the shoot-out victory on a one of the greatest nights in the history of the club.

After the match Parks kept his shirt and later gave it to his son, Joe. Tragically, Joe died in 2015 and Parks has loaned the shirt for inclusion in this book in his memory.

*Right: For the second leg of the final the word FINAL was added to the existing UEFA CUP 1983/84 embroidery. It is possible that this very shirt could have been worn in both legs of the final as well as the semi and quarter-finals (when the competition embroidery first appeared)*

# HUMMEL 1980s

## *Match shirt of* RAY CLEMENCE

In 1985 the Football League relaxed their rules concerning goalkeepers' shirts, removing the stipulation that they must be either green, blue, red or white and all one colour with no zips, buttons or other protrusions. This coincided with the arrival of Hummel as Tottenham Hotspur's kit suppliers and the Spurs goalkeeper's shirt would never be the same again.

Hummel's first two offerings were relatively understated, being in yellow – worn for the first time since the UEFA Cup in 1971 – and green, with contrasting collars and cuffs (black and white respectively). But by the end of the third Hummel season the company had unleashed no fewer than 10 different Spurs goalkeeper's shirts – of which we know at least seven were worn – which included grey, sky blue with navy sleeves and red *(right)*, although this was never worn in a first team match despite being match-prepared.

The early Hummel goalkeeper's shirts were actually straight out of the manufacturer's teamwear catalogue and on the blue example featured here *(far right)* you can see where a patch was created to cover the original sublimated manufacturer's logo on the right breast, with a new one embroidered higher up on the shirt. This was so that the logo would be visible on player headshots and in TV interviews.

With sublimation techniques improving, Hummel incorporated the diagonal pinstripes and horizontal band of chevrons as seen on the outfield player jerseys, and the No.1 on the back of the jerseys was also applied in this way.

For the final two season of the Hummel era, 1989–1991, things settled down and the company produced more traditional green and royal blue jerseys, although they included padded shoulders, elbows and forearms. Even these designs may have been a little racy for some traditionalists, but the message coming out of the kit manufacturers' design departments was: 'You ain't seen nothing yet.'

*After years of green goalkeeper's shirts, with the rules relaxed the floodgates opened and Hummel produced no fewer than 10 different styles for Ray Clemence to model*

# UMBRO 1990s

*Match worn by* ERIK THORSTVEDT

The tipping point for goalkeepers' shirt design came at the 1990 World Cup, when the likes of Colombia's Rene Higuita and Argentina's Sergio Goycochea sported outlandish and colourful patterned jerseys which upstaged the more traditional shirts worn by their opponents, effectively throwing the style guide out of the window.

When Umbro took over as Tottenham Hotspur's kit suppliers in 1991 they joined the party with a dark blue jersey featuring turquoise and pink flecks that was worn by Erik Thorstvedt in the 1991 FA Cup final. During the 1991/92 season Umbro produced four styles of goalkeeper's jersey for Spurs, with the yellow version of the same design being Thorstvedt's regular choice.

Also first worn in that first Umbro season (against Coventry) was the green 'Premier' style jersey which featured a cluster of triangles coming down the shoulders. Ten top-flight clubs used this style and there were numerous variations. A purple version was also worn twice during the 1991/92 campaign.

In 1992/93, with the advent of the Premier League, the referees' uniforms were changed to green – the default goalkeeper's shirt colour – and the gloves were truly off.

From the 1993/94 season Umbro were producing outlandish full goalkeeper's shirt, shorts and socks ensembles for most clubs (as opposed to the keepers wearing the same shorts and socks as the rest of the team). For 1994/95 they produced a variation of their truly off the wall 'Europa' jersey for Spurs which featured a garish turquoise and purple colour scheme complemented with a crazy pattern of triangles inspired by Umbro's double diamond logo.

*Popular Spurs keeper Erik Thorstvedt in action during the 1991 FA Cup final*

Clockwise from top left:

The first Umbro Spurs goalkeeper's jersey, one of four worn during the 1991/92 season (as well as the 1991 FA Cup final)

The Umbro 'Premier' style of jersey worn by no fewer than 10 top-flight clubs

A new Premier League rule introduced in 1994 allowed teams to name a goalkeeper as an extra third 'emergency' substitute. Many teams prepared additional outfield shirts so in the event of an injury when two subs had already been used they could bend the rules and bring on a goalkeeper as an outfield player. This, then, is the unused match shirt of Spurs' third-choice keeper Chris Day

The somewhat astonishing variation of the 'Europa' style jersey which lit up the 1994/95 season

# PONY 1990s

*Match shirt of* IAN WALKER

Umbro started the fashion for extremely lairy goalkeepers' shirts, but for many the Pony era jerseys (the company produced six in four years) pushed the boundaries of taste and style to the very limit. Two of the Pony offerings – one in green and yellow, the other in dark blue and orange – featured an obscure pattern of stars with matching shorts. Things calmed down a bit with this light-blue-and-orange-striped affair (worn between 1997 and 1999), which is perhaps the kit for which Ian Walker is best remembered. There was also a tamer green version of this design

# ADIDAS 1990s

*Match shirt of* IAN WALKER

Global kit brand adidas brought some order back to proceedings with some much simpler, calmer yellow, orange, green and black kits. The black one, pictured, was the first-choice home kit for the 1999/2000 season and will always be associated with Ian Walker. The smart black ensemble provided a welcome and stylish antidote to the Pony years

# KAPPA 2000s

*Match shirt of* PAUL ROBINSON

When stylish Italian brand Kappa took stewardship of the Spurs shirt in 2002, they pressed the reset button and went back to basics, not just with the home shirt but also the goalkeeper's jersey. Always simple and classically styled, Kappa produced kits in four different shades of green, orange, black and white, but the blue 2004/05 version pictured is the colour perhaps most associated with popular Spurs and England goalkeeper Paul Robinson

# PUMA 2000s

*Match shirt of* PAUL ROBINSON

With Puma, like Kappa who had come before them, it was a case of less is more with the two (or sometimes three) goalkeeper's kits they produced per season for Spurs between 2006 and 2012. Arguably the most stylish of the lot was this popular black jersey which was part of the 125th anniversary collection and regularly favoured by Paul Robinson

# UNDER ARMOUR 2010s

*Match shirt of* HUGO LLORIS

The range of goalkeeper's jerseys produced by Under Armour will always be associated with Hugo Lloris, who arrived at White Hart Lane at the same time as the American manufacturer in the summer of 2012.

The brilliant Frenchman seems to have a preference for bright, citrus colours. During his first season he generally favoured the yellow jersey over the green option and during the 2013/14 season he was regularly a highly visible presence in the bright orange 'HP' jersey *(below)*. He also continued to wear the yellow jersey from the previous season as a third shirt, with the new sponsor added.

During the 2014/15 season, Under Armour produced a simple but striking all-purple ensemble as part of their 'Echoes of Glory' collection which served as a tribute to the late, great Bill Nicholson. The signature pattern commemorating the 11 trophies that Tottenham Hotspur won under his stewardship, as seen inside the collar of the outfield players' shirts, appeared in the darker panels under the arms.

This purple strip – which earned Lloris the affectionate nickname of 'Barney' from the Spurs faithful on account of the colour being very similar to that of the loveable dinosaur TV character – was worn by the Spurs keeper during the 2015 Capital One Cup final defeat to Chelsea.

*Hugo Lloris consoles Jan Vertonghen after the 2-0 defeat to Chelsea in the 2015 Capital One Cup final*

CAPITAL ONE CUP FINAL
WEMBLEY STADIUM
1 MARCH 2015

AIA

# NIKE 2017/18

## *Match shirt of* HUGO LLORIS

When Nike took over as Tottenham Hotspur's kit manufacturer in 2017, they produced smart yellow and green kits – made using their 'Dri-Fit' technology – with a fading stripe effect running down the arms from the shoulders.

As is his wont, Lloris generally favoured the yellow jersey. However, no short-sleeved variation was ever produced for Spurs as the French international star generally prefers to wear long sleeves. There was also a black kit produced although this was never worn

The green version of Nike's first Spurs goalkeeper's shirt was not worn as often as the yellow jersey

# NIKE 2018/19

*Match shirt of* HUGO LLORIS

For Nike's second season, they produced a dazzling orange goalkeeper's jersey in line with the preference of Hugo Lloris for bright, citrus colours, as well as a stunning purple and lime green option guaranteed to make an impact.

The Gardien (in French the word for goalkeeper is 'gardien de but') jersey style was first unveiled for the 2018 World Cup in Russia where Lloris, as France captain, had lifted the World Cup in a yellow short-sleeved version of this Nike design

The orange version of the 2018/19 shirt was registered as the first choice for the Champions League

# INTO THE 21st CENTURY
## 2002–2012

KAPPA & PUMA

# HOME 2002-04

*Match worn by* LEDLEY KING

New owners, a new sponsor and a new kit supplier: these were watershed times at Tottenham. The takeover by ENIC in 2001 revitalised the club's commercial operation and one of the results was a new kit deal with Kappa, which Spurs supporter Simon Bamber – who was one of the driving forces behind the deal – had played a large part in rescuing in the late 1990s.

The Italian heritage brand had been in the business under various guises for almost a century, but it was best known in the UK for its adoption as a cult label by football fans influenced by the 'casuals' culture of the early 1980s. The company's 'Omini' logo, featuring a naked young man and woman sitting back-to-back in silhouette, added to its allure.

The shirt itself was a very clean, unfussy, plain white and featured a reverse-stitched seam using Kappa's radical 'Kombat 2002' technology – skin-tight polyamide lycra. This was another major sea-change in how kits were evolving, from baggy to tight fits. One aim of this change was to aid referees in spotting shirt pulling, but the real driving force was improved performance and player comfort. There's no doubt that it looked great on the team, but the same could not be said of all supporters… especially those who sported the XXL sizes and above.

The famous Kappa logo featured prominently on the right breast of the shirt, and the crest was of the same design as on the last adidas shirt. However, for the 2002/03 season there was a new sponsor with old and all but forgotten Tottenham links. Spurs had signed a reported £12 million deal with Thomson holidays, with the travel company's name detailed in red alongside parent company TUI's 'smiley' logo. Thomson was born out of a business created in the 1960s by a passionate Spurs fan, Aubrey Morris, who got into the industry after organising chartered air trips for fellow fans to see the team play abroad in the early days of European competition.

*Above: Ledley King in the club's first Kappa home shirt against Arsenal in December 2002*

*Right: Barclaycard Premiership sleeve patches were worn for one season only in 2003/04*

# AWAY 2002/03

*Match worn by* TEDDY SHERINGHAM

*Kappa's away shirt design featured an unusual navy and black colour combination, with contrasting sleeves and side panels. The reverse of the collar also featured a 'THFC' monogram*

# THIRD 2002/03

*Match worn by* JAMIE REDKNAPP

Yellow is a colour often associated with Spurs change kits, and the third shirt pictured here was given a bold and dynamic treatment that partially mirrored the home and away kits, this time with contrasting navy coloured side panels under each arm

# AWAY 2003/04

*Match worn by* TEDDY SHERINGHAM

The reverse-seams were non contrasting on the shirts for Kappa's second season, and improved ventilation was provided by increased mesh in the side panels. Spurs continued the trend of launching new kits in the last home game of the previous season, so this kit was actually first used in 2002/03 against Blackburn Rovers, which explains how it was worn by Teddy Sheringham in his final game for the club. The jersey is signed "304 – always a Spur" with the figure denoting the number of appearances he made for the club

# THIRD 2003/04

*Match worn by* JAMIE REDKNAPP

This third shirt was listed as purple, but in reality it was more of a shade of violet. It was an intriguing but successful choice of colour, and like its away shirt counterpart very minimalistic in style. All three shirts for the 2003/04 season carried the new Barclaycard Premier League sleeve badges, the first time a sponsor's name had appeared on these patches

# HOME 2004/05

*Match worn by* JERMAIN DEFOE

Kappa's second home shirt was an instant classic. It presented a cleaner, leaner proposition than their first effort and, but for some unavoidable concessions to modern styles and contractual obligations, delivered a jersey that fully embraced the Tottenham tradition.

It was the purest white shirt for decades, and the collar and cuff trim, as well as the reverse-seam stitching, were all non-contrasting. The shirt did not feature any tonal patterns, abstract shapes or detailing, apart from the 'SPURS' monogram embroidered in navy on the back of the collar. This was, almost by definition, a pure lilywhite home shirt, a direct homage to the Spurs kits of pre-1977, and its understated simplicity has arguably not received the retrospective acclaim it merits.

Made using Kappa's 'Kombat 2004' technology, the player shirts came with black and red 'GARA' tags on the side seams that indicated they were made from a lighter material composition compared to the one used for the replica shirts available to supporters. The fabric incorporated Kappa's moisture-managing technology and the sides also had mesh panels for ventilation.

Players and fans were now getting used to Kappa's sizing, although it helped that – perhaps with the replica shirt market in mind – this design had a baggier though more anatomical cut than the 2002 jersey.

The requisite club crest and manufacturer's logo were embroidred, but the Thomson logo – altered to include the company's new branding – was heat-applied vinyl. The club crest adhered to the template adopted in 1999, and there were new-style Barclays Premiership sleeve badges.

This unwashed Jermain Defore match worn shirt still shows the scars of battle, which would have ended its life as a first team shirt, although the exact match details are not known.

*Jermain Defoe wears the pure white 2004/05 Kappa home shirt against Norwich in September 2004. The shirt featured the new Barclays Premiership badges on the sleeves (right)*

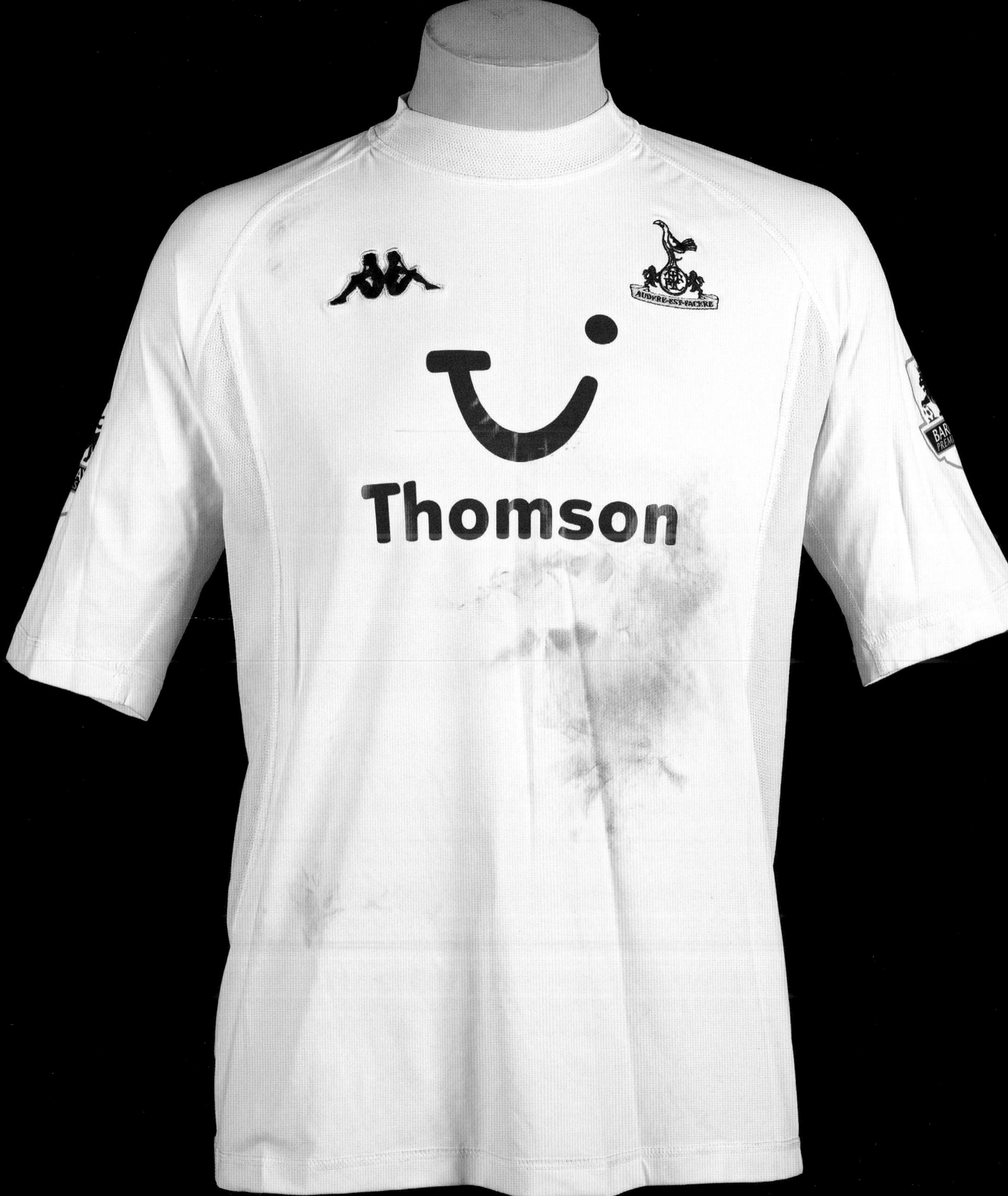
AUDERE EST FACERE
Thomson

# AWAY 2004/05

*Match worn by* SIMON DAVIES

Kappa's uncluttered home and away kits for the 2004/05 season were cleverly interchangeable if any clashes arose. All three together comprised arguably the best set of shirts the company produced. It was perhaps unfortunate, then, that this was the first season that the club launched three shirts to be used in only one campaign. This particular shirt saw action in the match away to Southampton on 5 March 2005

# THIRD 2004/05

*Match worn by* FREDI KANOUTE

The 2004/05 third shirt was a very bright yellow and challenged more conventional tastes. In all it was worn competitively seven times, four of those in domestic cup competitions

# HOME 2005/06

*Match worn by* EDGAR DAVIDS

As part of the cycle of releasing three kits per season, begun by Kappa the previous campaign, the company rang the changes for their final home shirt. The surprising addition of contrasting navy sleeves meant the shirt had echoes of the adidas 2002 Worthington Cup final shirt and its 1999 away predecessor, but this version represented a substantial break from tradition, especially following the clean and classic design of the previous season.

Apart from the navy sleeves, the overall design remained true to the now familiar Kappa style. The shirt had an unusual crew-neck-like collar, which included an insert strip across the front, while the 'SPURS' monogram on the back of the neck was removed from all three shirts for this season.

The sleeves, which were completed with white cuffs, extended to the shoulders in raglan style, and the navy motif was also extended down each side of the shirt to form sizeable panels which divided the front of the shirt from the back.

Another significant design change on the new shirt was the replacement of the popular 'Omini' logo with the branded wordmark of the manufacturer. From a collector's point of view, there were no obvious differences between the player and replica versions of this shirt – both now carried the 'GARA' tag – although the player shirts were originally manufactured in Italy.

Hugely experienced Dutch midfielder Edgar Davids represented another key signing for Tottenham as the club at last began to revitalise itself after a succession of managerial changes and an extended spell out of the race for major honours. Under the leadership of Martin Jol the club finished the 2005/06 season in fifth position, its highest placing since 1990.

*Dutch star Edgar Davids leaves Manchester United's Paul Scholes in his wake*

# AWAY 2005/06

*Match worn by* LEDLEY KING

Royal blue and trimmed with yellow side panels and a contrasting collar, this shirt was considered even starker in its rejection of convention than the corresponding home shirt. It was first worn in the Peace Cup against Real Sociedad bearing a 'Standard Chartered' logo, and only saw competitive action in four further games: at Grimsby Town, Bolton Wanderers, West Bromwich Albion and Fulham – with all four matches ending in defeat and Spurs failing to score on each occasion. This shirt was worn in the Bolton match on 7 November 2005

# THIRD 2005/06

*Match worn by* MICHAEL DAWSON

*The yellow and navy third shirt was only used twice, against Blackburn Rovers – against whom this shirt was worn by Michael Dawson in August 2005 – and later in the season against Wigan Athletic. It was almost a reverse of the home shirt, only lacking the contrasting colour side panels, and again featured navy sleeves and a non-contrasting collar. Kappa produced new away and third shirts every season, meaning that Spurs wore eight different away and third shirts over the course of their four-year contract, and there were 11 Kappa shirts in total*

# HOME 2006/07

*Match worn by* AARON LENNON

The end of the Kappa contract heralded the start of a new era and a brand-new kit supplier. Another company with German origins, Puma was born out of the acrimonious split between the founders of adidas – Adolf and Rudolf Dassler – in 1948, the latter forming the new company which quickly became adidas's greatest rival.

Spurs had struck a five-year deal with Puma to produce three shirts for each campaign as well as a one-off jersey for the club's 125th anniversary match. Their arrival also coincided with that of a new sponsor with Mansion, a gambling and entertainment group based in Gibraltar, committing to a four-year contract.

Puma's handsome first Spurs shirt was predominantly plain white with a non-contrasting crew-neck and cuffs. On the left breast the club crest was given a complete makeover, reverting to a more retro design with the club's latin motto removed altogether. This popular redesign of the club crest was a modern take on the classic badge that appeared on the club's shirts during the 1970s and early '80s. The cockerel was sleeker and more elegant, with the white head and neck giving way to a navy body, wings, legs and fighting spurs. In most instances this new crest, which was widely admired in design circles and warmly received by supporters, was to be used with the words 'Tottenham Hotspur' below the ball, but not on the shirt where the cleaner, simpler version was used.

In fact the shirt itself was not completely white. On the back was an arced blue shoulder panel that tapered down on each flank to a point, and within the collar was a heat-applied patch that read 'SPURS' in gold.

The long-sleeved version of the players' shirt had a different material applied to the forearms: a more breathable, elasticated fabric (with player comfort in mind) that was not found on the replica.

*Left: Pacy winger Aaron Lennon tussles with Arsenal's Emmanuel Adebayor in December 2006*

*Right: The damaged crest on this shirt, which was donated by Lennon to the Leeds Academy where he learnt his trade, shows either the scars of gameplay or the laundry process, giving it an impeccable match worn authenticity*

# AWAY 2006/07

*Match worn by* AARON LENNON

*The turquoise away shirt, a reverse of the home kit, was never worn in European competition and domestically was never worn in a winning game, its most positive outing coming in a draw at Fulham*

# THIRD 2006/07

*Match shirt of* DIMITAR BERBATOV

This shirt carried the new UEFA Cup sleeve patch

The arresting third shirt in chocolate with gold embellishment was produced in tribute to the 1895–1898 strip, with the gold crest inspired by White Hart Lane's actual cockerel statue. The Mansion logo was smaller on this European version of the shirt to comply with UEFA regulations. There was no real fanfare for the shirt's release, but 1,000 limited edition replica versions were put on sale ahead of a pre-season game against Inter Milan and immediately sold out. The long-sleeved version was never available as a replica. Originally intended for use as a cup kit only, it did actually make two outings in the league

# HOME 2007/08

*Match worn by* DIDIER ZOKORA

Tottenham were determined to do their 125th anniversary justice and a range of four Puma kits designed to pay tribute to the club's heritage and tradition were produced.

All four kits were launched simultaneously in May 2007, including a one-off blue-and-white-halved jersey to be worn in the club's official anniversary match against Aston Villa at the start of October.

All four shirts carried the bold monogram '125 Years' underneath the stylishly embroidered club crest and the clean, simple designs in the traditional Spurs colours are justifiably considered to be the high point of Puma's partnership with the club. The kit supplier had undoubtedly upped their game.

"They're excellent," enthused manager Martin Jol. "They look back at history and towards the future."

The 125th anniversary home jersey was a modern classic that paid homage to more than a century of lilywhite shirts, in particular emulating the shirt worn during the glory years of the late 1950s and early 1960s. Actually worn following the kit launch against Manchester City in the final game of the previous season, the home shirt sported a non-contrasting v-neck and cuffs. One modern touch was the tonal diagonal strips within the fabric, a special jacquard which contained the repeated text 'Tottenham Hotspur 125 Years 1882–2007'.

The only point of contention for some traditionalists was the coupling of white shorts in the style more often associated with European matches, but any dissenting voices were overshadowed by the positive response.

When the four shirts were first unveiled, Ian Connell from Puma UK said: "You're always nervous about showing players the new kits, but we always have to have confidence in what we do and we're pretty sure people are going to like what we show them." And people certainly did.

The Zokora shirt opposite actually carries the Premier League sleeve badges *(above right)* for the previous season as it was worn in the final match of the 2006/07 campaign – the design changed for the 2007/08 season.

*Above: Midfielder Didier Zokora – in blue shorts to avoid a clash – battles for possession against Portsmouth in December 2007*

*Top right: The 2007/08 season saw an update to the Premier League names and numbers which reverted back to navy and were slightly smaller*

*Above: The names and numbers used on the UEFA Cup shirts this season were in an unusual font designed by Puma*

# AWAY 2007/08

*Match worn by* DIMITAR BERBATOV

*Puma's design team considered this navy shirt as their strongest, design-wise, out of the set of 125th anniversary shirts. Worn five times during the season, it carried the same collar design as the anniversary shirt but without the contrasting colours*

# THIRD 2007/08

*Match worn by* JERMAIN DEFOE

The yellow third shirt was also worn on five occasions during the season, although it was never used in the UEFA Cup. It was never available for supporters to buy as a replica in long sleeves

The club's 125th anniversary season coincided with a revamp of the Premier League and a new lion design for the sleeve patches

# 125th ANNIVERSARY

## 1 OCTOBER 2007

It's always good to have something new to wear to a party, and Tottenham Hotspur's 125th anniversary celebration was very much one of those occasions. In keeping with the significance of the landmark, Puma produced a one-off shirt for the club's anniversary match, at home to Aston Villa on 1 October 2007, that was steeped in Spurs history.

The smart light-blue-and-white-halved shirt that Puma produced was based on the colour scheme of one of the club's earliest kits, one that was worn during the 1885/86 season and was originally donned in tribute to the dominant FA Cup-winning Blackburn Rovers side of the era.

Chairman Daniel Levy said: "Our 125th anniversary is a landmark for our club. Whilst our focus is always on providing for the future, it is equally important that we look to commemorate our long and rich heritage. A blue-and-white-halved shirt was first worn by our players in 1885 and a similar shirt will be worn on one occasion during the 2007/08 season to celebrate the club's 125th birthday."

Whatever the history, there was no doubting that the shirt was smart and stylish and, with White Hart Lane a sea of matching blue and white flags, the famous stadium was a colourful place indeed to be that night.

In keeping with the previous 125 years of the club's history, the match itself was a thrilling, topsy-turvy affair.

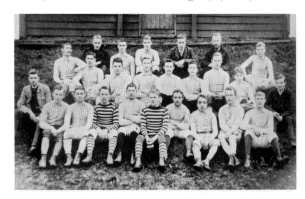

Out of form and in the relegation zone, Spurs found themselves 4-1 down after an hour and the atmosphere was decidedly flat. The away fans mocked the home support by ironically singing 'Happy Birthday', but just 30 minutes later the stadium was a riot of flag-waving colour and noise as Spurs salvaged a dramatic 4-4 draw in the final seconds.

Dimitar Berbatov had given the home side the lead, before the visitors did their best to upset the party. But then Pascal Chimbonda and Robbie Keane scored late goals, and just when a point looked unlikely Younes Kaboul levelled in stoppage time to provoke scenes of wild celebration.

Berbatov was one of only three players (the others being Chimbonda and Aaron Lennon) to wear the long-sleeved version of the shirt that was described as being 'reverse-halved' and had an alternating halved pattern on the sleeves. Only short-sleeved shirts were available to buy as replicas, which makes any long-sleeved match worn shirt especially rare and valuable.

The shirt was originally available for fans to buy in a limited edition box, complete with a numbered certificate of authenticity to commemorate the anniversary and make each one unique.

And even though he was injured and didn't play in the game, the club presented skipper Ledley King with his own numbered version and the legendary defender, now an ambassador for the club, lists it amongst his all-time favourite Spurs shirts. "I loved the 125th anniversary one," he said. "Even though I didn't play in the game, it was really special to me, and I've kept the one I was given."

An example of the shirt also took pride of place in the trophy cabinet sited in the club's 125 Room at the old White Hart Lane stadium, adjacent to the Oak Room in the West Stand. It was signed by the team that played against Aston Villa that night and donated to the club by then manager Martin Jol.

Left: Dimitar Berbatov punches the air in delight after giving Spurs the lead in their 125th anniversary match

Far left: The Tottenham Hotspur team is pictured (mostly) wearing light-blue-and-white-halved shirts in October 1885

Above: Younes Kaboul celebrates his late equaliser by removing his 'for one night only' jersey

# 125th ANNIVERSARY 2007

*Match worn by* DIMITAR BERBATOV

*Match worn by* ROBBIE KEANE

# LEAGUE CUP FINAL 2008

*Match worn by* JONATHAN WOODGATE

Played with the club's 125th anniversary as a backdrop, the 2007/08 season actually turned out to be one of considerable turmoil for Spurs. After the steady progress that had been built up under Martin Jol gave way to a serious loss of form and a perilous slide down the league table, the board opted for change and brought in former Sevilla manager Juande Ramos.

The managerial switch paid instant dividends as not only did Spurs move up the Premier League table but they reached another major final. Playing in the Carling-sponsored League Cup final meant that Tottenham would appear in their first showpiece Wembley final since 1999.

As was now the norm for cup finals, the shirts produced for the game carried specific match detail, 'Carling Cup Final' embroidered in the centre of the chest, along with the date of the game, '24 February 2008' underneath. This was the first time the full date of a cup final had ever appeared on a Spurs shirt. Competition-specific Carling Cup sleeve badges, dated 2008, adorned the sleeves but Premier League style letters and numbers were used.

The shirt pictured here was worn by match-winner Jonathan Woodgate, whose extra-time header gave Tottenham victory over favourites Chelsea and earned Spurs their first trophy for nine years.

The victory provided confirmation that the club was back on its recent upwardly mobile curve, competing for a top four league position and in the hunt for silverware on a more concerted basis than it had been for a generation.

*That winning feeling! Jonathan Woodgate celebrates with the Carling Cup trophy after his man of the match performance*

CARLING CUP FINAL
24 FEBRUARY 2008

125 YEARS

MANSION

# HOME 2008/09

*Match worn by* ROMAN PAVLYUCHENKO

The general trend of relatively simple Puma home shirts was bucked somewhat with this design, the company's third home jersey, which also represented the most concerted use of advanced fabric technology ever employed by the German kit supplier on a Spurs shirt.

The 2008/09 home shirt was, in effect, a modern-day version of the old Aertex shirts produced by Umbro in the 1970s. The overall design was still classic Tottenham, clean and simple lilywhite with navy trim but, unlike the replica shirts available in the club shop, those issued to the players used a dual-lined mesh fabric and incorporated a solid patch on the back to allow the application of letters and numbers. There was also an 'air pocket' hole on the front hem at the bottom of the shirt.

All of these features were Puma's response to the increasing popularity of base layers amongst players, showing that innovations in sportswear fabric and design could make a palpable difference to player comfort and, as a consequence, their sporting performance. These innovative developments only applied to the shirts the players wore which meant they were markedly different to the replica versions available for supporters to buy.

Outwardly, however, the player shirts and the replicas were still identical to the untrained eye. The shirt sported a neat navy shallow v-neck together with thin navy cuffs, while narrow navy panels were inserted into the sides. The kit reverted to navy shorts, along with unusual blue-and-white-hooped socks.

The club crest reverted to its now established modern design – losing the 125th anniversary embroidery– and the sponsor, Mansion, updated its branding to include the company's website address and the words 'Casino' and 'Poker', thus reducing the size of the main Mansion logo.

The mud-stained shirt featured here was worn by Roman Pavlyuchenko in the 0-0 home draw with Arsenal in February 2009.

*Above: Roman Pavlyuchenko on the ball against Arsenal at White Hart Lane*

*Top right: The length of Pavlyuchenko's name meant it had to be curved to make it fit*

*Above: Worn against Shakhtar Donetsk in the UEFA Cup, this Pascal Chimbonda shirt is significant (and rare) because the club registered the French full-back with a different number in European competition than he wore in the Premier League, 97 being the highest squad number ever used on a Spurs shirt*

# AWAY 2008/09

*Match worn by* AARON LENNON

The light blue away shirt was not one of Puma's most popular Spurs designs. On this shirt, worn in Europe by Aaron Lennon, the Mansion logo, complete with Mandarin lettering, is significantly smaller than on the domestic version to comply with UEFA's strict regulations

# THIRD 2008/09

*Match worn by* DIDIER ZOKORA

This shirt was something of a beauty – a Puma King commemorative-styled shirt which combined black with gold trim, plus a v-neck collar and twin Puma King stripes, making it a popular shirt which sold out extremely quickly. It was only worn five times, including one outing in Europe, and is a very rare and collectable shirt. This example was worn by Didier Zokora against Manchester City in November 2008

# LEAGUE CUP FINAL 2009

*Match worn by* LUKA MODRIC

Holders Spurs reached the League Cup final for the second season in succession, recovering from their stuttering early season form to continue the club's upward trajectory since the turn of the millennium.

The 2008/09 home shirt was customised for the final with centrally embroidered match detail similar to that of the previous season, but this time over three lines which incorporated the '1 MARCH 2009' date and also the text 'WEMBLEY STADIUM', as well as the 'Carling Cup 2009' sleeve badges. A limited edition replica of the shirt was available for fans to buy in the Spurs Megastore prior to the final.

Luka Modric, who had been signed in the summer of 2008, wore this jersey in the final, which ended in disappointment for Spurs who lost in a penalty shoot-out to Manchester United after the match finished 0-0 after 120 minutes.

Modric made a modest if encouraging start to his Spurs career during the course of his first campaign in lilywhite and blue, but he would go on to become the fulcrum of the side and arguably Tottenham's most influential midfielder since Paul Gascoigne.

The Croatian also presented a slightly different challenge for Sporting ID, the licensed manufacturer of the Premier League letters that made up the player names, as his surname required an accent above the letter 'c'.

*Midfield playmaker Luka Modric leaps over the challenge of Manchester United's Carlos Tevez during the 2009 Carling Cup final*

CARLING CUP FINAL
WEMBLEY STADIUM
1 MARCH 2009

MANSION.COM
CASINO & POKER

# HOME 2009/10

*Match worn by* TOM HUDDLESTONE

Puma's designs had up until now been aesthetically pleasing if not a little restrained, but the 2009/10 season's home shirt saw the manufacturer take the traditional lilywhite jersey in a whole new direction.

Yellow had always been seen as the third Spurs colour, primarily for use on away shirts and only ever used with subtlety on home shirts. But when Puma unveiled this shirt, on which yellow detail was extremely prominent, opinion among the fans was divided.

The shirt earned the nickname the 'wing shirt' due to the two yellow strips that formed a wide 'v' pattern extending from the top of the chest to the shoulders, and then around the back to join up with the yellow side panels. It was undoubtedly unlike any Spurs shirt seen before or since.

Above this yellow trim on the chest was a 'yoke' neckpiece that was unique to every shirt. It featured random sections of grey and white patterned material, rendered individual by the cut of the cloth in the factory, which was akin to each shirt having its own unique fingerprint. The 'yoke' adjoined a plain white crew-neck on the front and back.

Over the top of each shoulder was a navy leaping Puma logo, smaller in size than the more traditional manufacturer's logo on the right breast, and there was a navy trim that ran down the lower portion of the yellow side panels and along the hem of the shirt. This trim also formed thin navy cuffs.

Whilst not universally popular, the shirt is affectionately remembered for some of the memorable performances in which it saw action. This shirt was worn by midfielder Tom Huddlestone for the famous 2-1 victory over Arsenal, in which full-back Danny Rose scored a sensational screamer on his Premier League debut. The style was also worn for the win at Manchester City that earned Tottenham their first-ever Champions League qualification.

*Midfielder Tom Huddlestone in the unusual 2009/10 home shirt which split opinion amongst Spurs fans*

# AWAY 2009/10

*Match worn by* JERMAINE JENAS

The away shirt, which was worn three times in the run to the FA Cup semi-finals, was almost an exact reverse of the home design but featured only two colours and incorporated a different collar design. It also carried the Mandarin script that had appeared on recent away shirts. This shirt was worn by Jermaine Jenas against Bolton in October 2009

# THIRD 2009/10

*Match worn by* NIKO KRANJCAR

This was another popular Puma King tribute third shirt, with its two stripes giving it something of a continental feel. It also included a tonal diagonal shadow pattern and a wrapover collar

# LEST WE FORGET

In November 2009 the Spurs team ran out for the home fixture against Sunderland with a poppy emblem on the left breast of their shirts for the first time. Tottenham were amongst a small number of Premier League clubs to make this tribute to those who made the ultimate sacrifice for their country, but a year later all 20 clubs and most others in the professional game were adorning their jerseys with the traditional symbol of remembrance. Spurs have subsequently worn a poppy on their shirts for the fixture closest to Remembrance Sunday every year since.

The poppy became a symbol of tribute to the fallen after Canadian surgeon John McCrae's 1915 poem *In Flanders Fields*, referencing the red poppies that grew over the graves of fallen soldiers and flowered on the war-ravaged landscape. It was adopted for the Royal British Legion's annual Poppy Appeal in 1921, and has since been worn to honour servicemen and women who have lost their lives in all conflicts since the First World War, but also as a symbol of new life.

Since 2009, in support of the Poppy Appeal, Tottenham's match worn 'Poppy Shirts' have been signed by the players and auctioned, with the proceeds donated to the charity, as well as Help For Heroes. Some shirts have sold for staggering amounts.

For the first three years the poppy became a 'lucky' emblem for Spurs, with wins against Sunderland, Blackburn and Fulham. This sequence ended with defeat at Manchester City in 2012, a match that started a run of three successive losses in the poppy shirt, including reverses against Newcastle and Stoke at White Hart Lane. In the 2015/16 and 2016/17 seasons the 'Poppy Shirt' weekend coincided with the North London Derby, with both matches ending in 1-1 draws.

*Left: Spurs wore the poppy for the first time against Sunderland on 7 November 2009*

*Above: The poppy design from the 2015/16 shirt*

*Right:*
*1. v Sunderland – home (7 November 2009)*
*2. v Blackburn Rovers – home (13 November 2010)*
*3. v Fulham – away (6 November 2011)*
*4. v Manchester City – away (11 November 2012)*
*5. v Newcastle – home (10 November 2013)*
*6. v Stoke – home (9 November 2014)*
*7. v Arsenal – away (8 November 2015)*
*8. v Arsenal – away (6 November 2016)*
*9. v Crystal Palace – home (5 November 2017)*

1.

2.

3.

4.

5.

6.

7.

8.

9.

# HOME 2010/11

*Match worn by* AARON LENNON

The penultimate home shirt of the Puma era again saw some significant changes, with another adventurous design coinciding with a new commercial era for the club that saw different sponsors appear on the shirts for different competitions.

The club's main sponsor was now Autonomy – a software and IT services company later bought by previous Spurs sponsor Hewlett-Packard – although the Autonomy name and logo only featured on the shirt for league matches. Tottenham had struck an innovative sponsorship deal, enabling them to negotiate contracts with different partners for cup competitions (for this season it was Investec). Importantly, this helped Spurs to maximise the commercial opportunities presented by the club's first-ever season in the Champions League.

The fabric of the shirt itself included diagonal strips that were actually perforations designed for ventilation and player comfort. But the most distinctive feature was the navy panel that ran across the shoulders, tapering from a broader panel on the right shoulder to a narrower band on the left. Within this design feature appeared an alternating navy and white stripe detail, while the Puma logo was picked out in white and positioned high on the right shoulder. This meant that it was now placed higher than the club crest, which was not a universally popular development. On the back, the navy panel was extended in a semi-circle below the white collar.

The jersey also featured a white wrapover contemporary crew-neck collar with an inserted white 'v' detail bisecting the navy shoulder panel to the front.

The shirt pictured here was worn by electric winger Aaron Lennon against Liverpool on 28 November 2010, a match in which he scored the last-minute winner.

*Aaron Lennon runs with the ball during the clash between Tottenham Hotspur and Liverpool at White Hart Lane in November 2010 – the game in which the shirt featured here was worn*

# AWAY 2010/11

*Match shirt of* TOM HUDDLESTONE

The sky blue away shirt for 2010/11 featured alternate navy and white trim on the front of the shoulders and upper arms, as well as an unusual collar that made it particularly distinctive

The only time the shirt was worn with an Investec sponsor was against Fulham in the FA Cup, where it also lacked any competition sleeve badges

# THIRD 2010/11

*Match worn by* LUKA MODRIC

The navy third shirt was a very busy design with a complicated collar and the introduction of lime green, the first time this colour had ever been used on a Spurs shirt. It also included the addition of white flashes, bars and trims. Luka Modric wore this shirt against Real Madrid in the Champions League in November 2011

# HOME CHAMPIONS LEAGUE 2010/11

*Match worn by* GARETH BALE

Qualifying for the Champions League had become something of a holy grail for Spurs, who had not taken part in UEFA's premier club tournament since 1962 despite several near misses, so this shirt is fondly remembered for the memorable European campaign in which it was worn and particularly the marauding brilliance of Welsh star Gareth Bale, whose two performances against Inter Milan will never be forgotten.

Bale, who truly announced his talent to a global audience with his extraordinary turn in the 4-3 defeat away to Inter Milan in an October 2010 Champions League group stage match, was the undoubted star of Tottenham's run to the quarter-finals. The shirt pictured here was worn by Bale in his perhaps even more impressive match-winning display in the home match against Inter, where he famously tore the Internazionale defence to shreds, in particular full-back Maicon, who was subjected to chants of 'Taxi for Maicon' by the White Hart Lane faithful.

The shirts used in European competition had some noticeable difference to those worn in the Premier League. On the right sleeve the Champions League 'starball' logo appeared prominently, and UEFA's 'RESPECT' campaign badge appeared on the left sleeve, both produced in flock 'SensCilia' material.

On the front, cup sponsor Investec's logo was printed in vinyl and as large as UEFA rules allowed. The logo that appears on this Bale shirt is the final incarnation of three versions trialled during the 2010/11 season. The kit was completed with the white shorts and socks befitting Tottenham's European traditions, albeit the right leg of the shorts carrying a diagonal blue flash that mirrored that seen on the shoulders of the shirt.

The new Spurs-specific letter and number font on the back was used on all three cup kits, both in the Champions League and domestic cup competitions, the sole difference being that the small club crest in the base of the numbers only appeared on shirts worn in Europe.

*Above: Gareth Bale, pictured in the shirt featured here, during perhaps his greatest performance in a Spurs shirt – at home to Inter Milan in the 2010 Champions League*

*Above right: Spurs' 2010 Puma shirt was the first to be adorned by the Champions League 'Starball' logo and the UEFA 'Respect' badge*

# HOME 2011/12

*Match worn by* RAFAEL VAN DER VAART

The final Puma home shirt of their four-year Tottenham contract went back to basics with a more traditional plain, simple and unfussy design featuring pure unadulterated lilywhite. It did not contain any quirky design features or styling. There were no piping details, frills or flashes, and no contrasting trims – and it worked a treat.

In keeping with the more traditional overall design approach, the most discernable difference from previous recent shirts was the understated retro collar reminiscent of the style worn during the mid-1950s.

Another new feature was the shirt sponsor which, conversely, signified something altogether more modern. In fact the actual sponsor was still Autonomy, but for this season the branding for the company's latest innovation, Aurasma, took pride of place on the front of Spurs' Premier League jerseys. Aurasma, a so-called 'augmented reality platform', provided a unique extra dimension to the new shirt. The app recognises images and objects viewed through a smartphone or tablet's cameras and overlays interactive multimedia content such as videos – dubbed 'Auras' – on top of them to enhance the user's experience. By pointing a suitably enabled smartphone at the shirt, fans were able to watch footage of Tottenham goals, interviews and behind-the-scenes news.

The cup version of the jersey carried the now familiar Investec logo and – for the first time in European competition – the Europa League badges appeared on the right sleeve while the UEFA 'Respect' badges that had previously been seen in the Champions League season were affixed to the left.

All in all this was a fine shirt for Puma to bow out with. The Premier League jersey pictured here was worn by Rafael van der Vaart, a modern Spurs cult hero who thrilled supporters with his huge repertoire of skills and several crucial goals.

*Above: Rafael van der Vaart celebrates scoring against Blackburn Rovers at White Hart Lane in April 2012*

*Right: Europa League patches appeared on the Spurs shirt for the first time*

*Above: The Investec version of the shirt was used in Tottenham's first-ever Europa League campaign*

# AWAY 2011/12

*Match worn by* GARETH BALE

All three shirts for the 2011/12 season had very different collar styles. The lilac away shirt featured a plain white contrasting crew-neck with white contrasting cuffs. The Aurasma shirt pictured here was worn by Gareth Bale against Stoke City, the only time he wore a long-sleeved version of this jersey, and even then he only wore it for 45 minutes as he changed into short sleeves at half-time

The jersey was never worn in domestic cups with Investec on the front – the cup version only being worn in the Europa League

# THIRD 2011/12

*Match worn by* MASSIMO LUONGO

The third shirt, with its gold diagonal Puma King motif, was worn in only two cup games with Investec as the title sponsor: against Stevenage in the FA Cup fifth round and in a League Cup penalty shoot-out defeat to Stoke in which Massimo Luongo, making his only senior appearance for Spurs, missed the deciding spot-kick

The Aurasma version was worn in the league away at Swansea, Blackburn, QPR and Bolton

# GUARDIANS OF THE SHIRT

To many supporters, especially kit enthusiasts and shirt collectors, from the outside the position of kit man at Tottenham Hotspur Football Club would appear to be a dream job. You would be close to your heroes, an integral part of the inner sanctum of the dressing room, working for your club and in charge of the kit. Easy. But of course it's not quite that simple.

For a start, at a modern Premier League football club the job is now kit manager – not kit man – and that individual is in charge of a whole team of people tasked with preparing and organising match and training kit for numerous teams. There are different shirt numbers and sleeve badges for all the various competitions, sponsor logos of varying sizes for different matches and kits to pack up and ship all over the world. Nowadays it is a huge operation.

However, you don't have to travel too far back in time to find a completely different world. In the days before the Premier League, clubs generally muddled through, the kit man job being shared with a number of other roles.

No club succeeds without good backroom staff and the kit men and their colleagues in the laundry room are integral members of that team. They are unsung heroes, their importance to the atmosphere of the dressing room and the morale of the team often overlooked. Kit men are a vital component in achieving togetherness and harmony amongst the squad, often being closer to the players than any other member of staff and considered the main link between the dressing room and management.

Incredibly, since Spurs employed their first full-time kit man in 1974, only three people have held the job at Tottenham Hotspur. Former groundstaff member Roy Reyland held the post between 1987 and 2007, before handing the keys to the kit room over to his assistant, Steve Dukes, who is currently Head of Kit/Equipment Logistics.

But the kit man role at Spurs is synonymous with one of the club's truly legendary characters…

# THE KING OF THE KIT ROOM

*Previous pages: Tottenham Hotspur home and away shirts are hung out to dry prior to the start of the 1934/35 season. In comparison, looking after the current Spurs kit is a massive logistical operation*

*Far right: Club legend Johnny Wallis had an influence on the dressing room that went far beyond his stated role of kit man*

*Below right: Wallis with manager Keith Burkinshaw and the FA Cup following the club's victory in 1982*

The first man formally employed in the kit man role by the club, Johnny Wallis looked after the Spurs shirt for more than 30 years. He was a Tottenham Hotspur institution. He joined the club in 1936 as an amateur player, having already captained representative school sides and played for England Schoolboys. War interrupted his progress and ultimately injury put paid to his hopes of a professional playing career. Returning to north London, Wallis took coaching and medical courses at Birmingham University and, allied to his playing experience, put them to expert and dedicated use at Spurs over the course of the next five decades.

Wallis did virtually every job going at White Hart Lane: successful A team and then reserve team manager, trainer and physio until, in 1974, he was officially appointed kit manager. In reality he had already been doing the job for more than 15 years as part of his backroom role – ordering kit, repairing shirts, looking after the players' boots, preparing the strip for training and matches and generally making it his personal obsession to ensure that the players

were always decked out in pristine, lilywhite kit befitting the class and style of Tottenham Hotspur Football Club.

Wallis had a reputation for being a chronic hoarder. While brand-new shirts and shorts lay unused in boxes, players would train in tatty kit. It stemmed from the more frugal post-war days during which Wallis was reared, adhering to a scrupulous 'waste not, want not' ethos that was shared by many a kit man of this era.

He developed a unique organisational code for each set of shirts that involved marking the bottom hem with a system of dots, dashes and letters relevant to the team they were to be used for. New shirts of course went to the first team, and then they were handed down to the reserves, the A and youth teams. Eventually they became training kit before finally being cut up into rags and given to apprentices to carry out their cleaning duties. Wallis' system and his strict adherence to it is one of the reasons so few shirts from the 1960s, '70s and '80s have survived.

Wallis ran the kit room like a well-oiled machine. Training kit had to be washed and transported from the laundry room at White Hart Lane to the training ground at Cheshunt every day. Match kit had to be washed, dried and laid out before every game, home and away. Wallis had his coding system and various routines but there were no notebooks or spreadsheets – it was all in his head.

Former manager Keith Burkinshaw has fond memories of Wallis both as a friend and as a man who was very good at his job: "With Johnny, everything was right, for every game. I never had to worry about the kit, it was just done."

Club historian John Fennelly knew Wallis well, first as a Tottenham fan living close to the Cheshunt training ground, then as a journalist before he joined the club full-time as press officer.

"All the shirts were the same size no matter what your height or physique. If you were given a particular number for a match, that's what you wore. John Pratt talks about how he was acknowledged as a hard worker because of the image he portrayed with his sleeves rolled up. But he only

## "JOHNNY WALLIS WAS THE HEART AND SOUL OF THE DRESSING ROOM"
### KEITH BURKINSHAW

did it because otherwise those orangutan sleeves would have dragged along the pitch as he ran!

"Johnny religiously guarded his kit, right down to the tie ups. He counted everything out and he counted everything back in again. He had gear going back decades and wouldn't even lend you a sock with a hole in."

Steve Perryman remembers: "One of the best jobs as an apprentice was cleaning Johnny's kit room . There would be boxes and boxes of brand-new kit all over the place but we were running around training in tatty old rags."

All of this is backed up by every ex-player you talk to, from the likes of club stalwart Graham Roberts to former loanee goalkeeper Martin Thomas, with Tony Galvin commenting: "He treated the kit like it was his own. He'd take it as a personal affront if you took anything or, even worse, if you lost anything."

Martin Chivers recalls an occasion early on in his Spurs career when he pulled on his shirt and "the sleeves came halfway up my forearms". "It was miles too small," says the club's strapping former No.9, "but Johnny wasn't going to change the shirt and told me to just get on with it." It wasn't until Bill Nick walked in and said "just give him another one Johnny" that he was finally forced to give Chivers a new shirt.

After an impressive debut as a 17-year-old against Stoke City in 1979, former striker Terry Gibson discovered how protective of the Spurs kit Wallis was after he was left bloodied, battered and with a ripped shirt by the opposition defenders. Fennelly recalls that, whilst working as a reporter for the *Tottenham Weekly Herald*: "I interviewed Terry the following Monday, asking if he had the shirt for a photograph? 'No', he sulked. 'Johnny Wal took it back and had it bleached and repaired!'"

Wallis zealously guarded his kit room and its contents. Laundry manager Sylvie Webb recalls Terry Yorath having to climb in through the hatch that linked the laundry with Wallis' deadlocked lair to liberate his 'TY' tracksuit.

But Wallis was much, much more than just a kit man. He kept the confidences of both club and players, and knew when they should be shared. Keith Burkinshaw described him as "the heart and soul of the dressing room".

He was a vital cog in the backroom machine – keeping players on their toes, from seasoned first teamers to wide-eyed apprentices, and generally ruling the training ground with an iron fist… albeit with a twinkle in his eye.

Wallis certainly had a dry sense of humour. At face value he could be intimidating, and not just to callow apprentices. "He was a great man but, yes, also very scary," laughs Ricky Villa. But behind the gruffness was a dedicated perfectionist who cared deeply about his job and the people he worked with.

## WALLIS WAS MUCH, MUCH MORE THAN JUST A KIT MAN. HE WAS A VITAL COG IN THE BACKROOM MACHINE

He was tough on the players, particularly the apprentices, of whom in those days the kit man was in charge. It was toughness with a deliberate purpose – to test the character of aspiring players. If they could not withstand the Wallis treatment, what hope would they have in the ferment of professional football?

"If you cheat at your jobs, I'm telling you, you will cheat on the pitch," Perryman remembers being one of Wallis' favourite sayings.

"He was intimidating but equally engaging and was always there to offer advice," is Micky Hazard's memory of 'The Wal', while former apprentice goalkeeper Tony Parks remembers a favourite Wallis saying being, "The day I stop moaning at you is the day I stop caring."

Perryman sums Wallis up as "one of the cornerstones of Tottenham Hotspur" and Hazard describes him as "a proper Spurs character who gave his heart and soul to the club".

In tandem with laundry manager Sylvie Webb, Wallis ensured that the Spurs shirt was immaculate for nearly 30 years, and the pair were a stable element at the club through a period of huge change in the 1980s. Not all of the modern developments in the game were to Wallis' liking. Unsurprisingly he was not a fan of players exchanging shirts – "He wasn't too pleased when it happened because he'd have to order new ones," says Sylvie – and the 1987 FA Cup final episode, when a mix-up saw half the team run out in shirts missing the logo of the club's main sponsor, inevitably hurt a man who prided himself on his perfectionism. "I really felt for Johnny after that, it wasn't really his fault," Richard Gough, skipper for the occasion, recalls.

But as Wallis wound down his Tottenham career, receiving an MBE for his services to football in 1993, he had left a legacy any successor would be hard-pressed to emulate.

*Below: More than a kit man! Johnny Wallis (second left) shouts instructions from the Spurs bench during the 1970s when Terry Neill (third from the right) was manager*

# THE LEGEND OF THE LAUNDRY ROOM

Another highly respected and much-loved figure at the club, Sylvie Webb ran the White Hart Lane laundry room with precision and organisation for 28 years – from 1970 until 1998 – managing the huge daily operation to wash and repair the daily mountains of muddy football kit.

"I worked with 10 managers, I think," says Sylvie (it was actually 13 plus four caretaker managers), who lived a Pat Jennings' goal kick from the stadium and even in retirement is still as north London as they come, with warmth and a pin-sharp wit to match. "There was Bill Nick, Terry Neill, Keith Burkinshaw, Peter Shreeves, Terry Venables, Ossie Ardiles,

Christian Gross… and that one from Arsenal, who used to wear a mac. What was his name?"

Sylvie talks with a chuckle and a twinkle in her eye, giving an insight into how, just like Johnny Wallis, her influence at Spurs went far beyond her job title and right to the very heart and soul of the club. She became a vital member of the backroom team, an essential ingredient in the day-to-day chemistry of the club with a combination of motherly care and reliable efficiency helping to guide several generations of players, and indeed managers, through their careers in London N17.

*Above: Sylvie Webb (background) and her team of Liz Thorpe (left) and Shirley Ravenall (right) hard at work as usual in the White Hart Lane laundry room in 1988*

Sylvie arrived at Spurs in the summer of 1970 when the decision was made to bring the laundering of the kit in-house. Outsourcing the laundry – a common practice amongst football clubs at the time – had been costing the club £7,000 a year and the service was not up to scratch. "The shirts had marks on them," she remembers, "and the players used to have to turn the socks the wrong way out to put them on. Mud and grass would fall out of them."

With the club's first full-time 'laundry lady' in charge, the Spurs shirt would soon return to dazzling lilywhite. A combination of teamwork, superb organisational skills and tricks-of-the-trade ensured that the Spurs team always looked magnificent during Sylvie's three decades of service.

"I used to just do my best, and get the shirts as white as I could. I must say that none of my shirts ever went out with mud on them, or with marks, not at all. I wouldn't allow it. They couldn't go out like that.

"Quarter to eight, I'd get in every morning. You'd sort all the work out. You'd try and get the reserves and first team shirts in one machine, to get as many as you could done there and then. Towels were the hardest things to get dry, so I would try to get them in quick, in the dryer, and then the next batch, so it was all done within one day, dried and finished. When I shut that door, everything was done. I didn't want anything hanging over until the next day, because then it built up come Friday. But if they played on Saturday, and had an away game on Wednesday, I would go in after the match and put the kit in to soak; Sunday morning I would wash them, and get them ready to be packed up and taken away. So, they were basically done by the Monday."

But some days the job was harder than others. "Leeds," exclaims Sylvie with her eyes raised to the ceiling. "When the boys played there you could never get the shirts clean. They were terrible. Don't know what they put in the soil in Leeds, it was awful to try to get the shirts clean. But we did in the end. I found that if I used Fairy Liquid and a scrubbing brush, I was able to get them clean."

# SYLVIE WEBB WAS A VITAL INGREDIENT IN THE DAY-TO-DAY CHEMISTRY OF THE CLUB

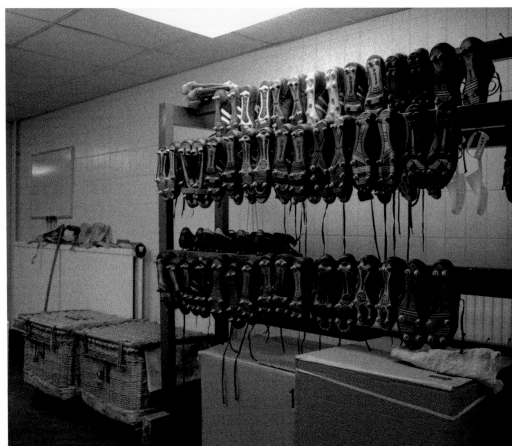

*Above: The home dressing room at White Hart Lane, all ready and prepared (including a long-sleeved shirt for left-back Mitchell Thomas) for a match during 1988*

*Left: The players' boots, prepared and ready to go, before the same match*

*Above, right: Sylvie Webb hard at work in the laundry room in 1971 (above) – in the days before she managed a whole team (below)*

*Following pages: Work begins on tackling the daily mountain of kit that would go through the laundry room every day*

The Admiral kit of the 1970s was also problematic. "We couldn't get the socks clean, so Keith Burkinshaw got Admiral down. They said that I was to only wash them at 30 degrees. Well, I done them on 30, hung them up, and Burkinshaw – I got on really well with him – walked into the laundry, saw they were still not clean and said, 'What the bloody hell's going on here?' I said, 'Well, I've washed them just like I was told.' 'Take them down and do them your way,' he said."

This pride extended to the cleaning of all the club's kit, including the players' training kit, which of course during the season needed washing virtually every day. She recalls that when she first started at Tottenham, dirty training kit was simply hung out to dry on hot water pipes. "Oh, it smelt horrible. And when it was all dry they just used to wear whatever was available, including the jockstraps. So when I started, I made sure that each player had two clean sets every day that they trained. I didn't think it was nice, wearing somebody else's socks and jockstrap."

But Sylvie's role at the club went far beyond washing the kit. The White Hart Lane laundry room was located in a corner close to the car park by the players' entrance outside the West Stand, and it provided a welcome alternative environment to the strict and very macho world of the dressing room and training ground. She and her colleagues created a caring, maternal environment that drew everyone, from managers to apprentices, into her welcoming domain. As the original King of White Hart Lane, Alan Gilzean, explained: "Johnny Wallis' room was permanently locked, but there was always a warm welcome from Sylvie in the laundry room."

Micky Hazard's memories echo Gilzean's sentiments: "When I was an apprentice I was always trying to get out of my jobs and Sylvie and the other laundry ladies would make the laundry room a warm and friendly place to congregate – they were fantastic people."

With club-provided supplies of tea, coffee and milk, and a kettle rarely off the boil, she made endless cuppas for all who popped their heads round the laundry room door for a chat. Hazard says: "It was an intimate place where everybody felt comfortable," and Tony Parks, another former apprentice, adds: "Sylvie was a lovely lady, she was just brilliant. Even when we were a bit cheeky, she'd look after us apprentices like a second mum."

Even the managers were frequent visitors. "Bill Nick always had a cup – and I mean a cup – of tea. Bill had the

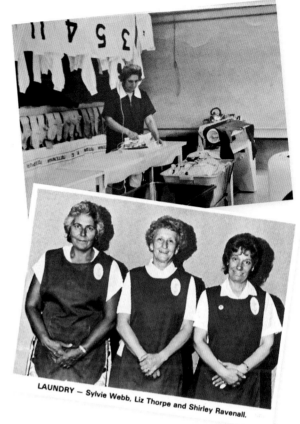

LAUNDRY — Sylvie Webb, Liz Thorpe and Shirley Ravenall.

shakes a bit. He'd say, 'I don't want that bloody thing' and the saucer would be put down, and he would just have the cup. He was a nice manager. He was really strict, and very traditional. I used to wear trousers, which he didn't like. 'What have you got bloody trousers on for?' 'Well,' I said, 'because of having to bend over the trollies and bins; I can't be doing that out in the car park with a skirt on, can I?' So he went, 'Oh, all right then.'

"One day, we'd had a lot of rain, and Bill Nick comes in and says, 'Webby' – he called me Webby – 'come with me, and bring half a dozen of those big bed sheets.' We went out there and, at the end of the tunnel there was a dip on to the pitch and that part of it was sodden. I nearly had a fit! He laid the sheets on the puddles and said, 'Stamp on them with me.' So, we stamped on all these sheets to mop this water up so a match could go on. Then he said, 'Right, get those as white as when they come out!' It took a bit of time, but I did."

"Terry Venables was the only manager who asked me into his office when he was ordering some kit. He'd never done it before. Ooh, the language. 'How the f***** hell do I know what to order?' he said, 'Well I don't know, I've never ordered it. The managers always do it.'"

For the players who went through the club there was, and still is, universal love for Sylvie. Steve Perryman invited her and her husband Alf to sit at his table for his 40th birthday party. And when Sylvie finally called it a day in 1998, Paul Miller wrote to her saying: "I remember those early morning cups of tea; I used to sneak in when Johnny Wallis wasn't looking. You've been a fantastic help to many of the young lads over the years, not least myself. I'm sure we're all thankful for your little bit of guidance along that rough, rocky road that eventually leads to playing with the first team and winning things".

That laundry room welcome was extended to all ages. "When Colin Calderwood was going in [for treatment]," says Sylvie, "he often brought his little boy, Alfie, into the laundry. We had a linen basket and we used to stick the little 'un in the there, give him a biscuit to keep him quiet, and carried on with our work while Colin was having his treatment".

The kindness was reciprocated. Another Colin, Sylvie's son, often went with her to the ground, particularly in the school holidays. and became very much part of the White Hart Lane scenery.

"It's how I got all the players' autographs," Colin explains. "The door to the boot room was right there next to Mum's laundry door, so I used to just tuck myself in there".

As he got older, Colin was taken under the wing of Wallis. He would travel with the legendary kit man to the training ground at Cheshunt to help out. He was even put in goal one day before training proper started, with Pat Jennings lashing a spot kick which the youngster just about got a hand to. "My fingers are still tingling," he says, smiling at the memory.

Before the 1972 UEFA Cup final, an eight-year-old Colin was invited by Wallis to help put out the kit for the second leg at White Hart Lane. All week there had been speculation over whether or not Alan Mullery would play. Whilst Colin was in the dressing room fetching the players' boots and

shin pads, Bill Nick came in and gave the team sheet to Wallis, which revealed that Mullery was indeed starting. After nipping back home Colin – sworn to the utmost secrecy by Wallis – and his dad Alf walked to the stadium for the match, with father imploring son to divulge if 'Mullers' was playing. Ever dutiful to the Spurs cause, Colin kept resolutely quiet.

Colin was the lucky recipient of a handful of mementos from his mother's time at Spurs. One of a few Wallis personally saved for Colin was Richard Gough's damaged shirt from 1987 with its huge tear down the front, while as a child his mum would sometimes bring home prototype shirts which he'd try on before they were whisked back to White Hart Lane. Ever proud of his mum's contribution to his team's history and the respect she still commands today from so many former players, when somebody recently complained to Colin that their mother had ruined his replica Le Coq Sportif shirt by using an iron, he quickly replied: "If my mum hadn't known how to use an iron she could have changed Tottenham Hotspur's history".

The camaraderie and the jokes in the laundry room were understandably lively. The laundry ladies had no time for reputation and could be mercilessly unforgiving. One player in particular rubbed them up the wrong way.

"I kept getting these red socks in with the training kit," recalls Sylvie. "I went mad, because the red kept washing out into everything else. I found out who it was and I says, 'Don't put them in the wash no more.' 'Why not?' he said. 'Because they're making everything else go red and I don't want it. If they come in again, I'm binning them,' I said".

Asked to volunteer the name of the offending player, Sylvie thinks a while before confirming it was Sol Campbell.

"'You can't do that, they belong to me,' he said. But they didn't come back any more. He never spoke to me after that, mind," she says with a wry smile.

Manufacturers came and went – Sylvie worked on the kit produced by six different suppliers – but she and her system remained largely unchanged, although there was a huge increase in the amount of work once the Premier League came in. "In the old days you'd sort the shirts by the numbers, No.1-11. Sometimes if it was wet or someone got injured, they would have another shirt. But most times, it was just one shirt for one person".

But if Sylvie's job looking after the Spurs shirt became harder, she was not one to make a fuss. "It was just a great job," she smiles.

## "THERE WAS ALWAYS A WARM WELCOME FROM SYLVIE IN THE LAUNDRY ROOM"
ALAN GILZEAN

# BORN IN THE USA
## 2012–2017

UNDER ARMOUR

# HOME 2012/13

*Match worn by* GARETH BALE

The agreement with American company Under Armour to become Tottenham's new kit supplier heralded the arrival of a major player in sports apparel looking to establish itself in the British football market. Spurs became the company's first club and the forerunner for Under Armour's European ambitions.

Founded in 1996 by former university athlete Kevin Plank, Under Armour was at the time better known for its pioneering base layer – close-fitting performance sportswear – products but in recent years had branched out into stylised player clothing for sports like tennis and golf before targeting the football market.

For its first Spurs shirt the company used an aesthetically pleasing lightweight fabric incorporating the company's 'Heatgear' technology – Under Armour's signature moisture transport system that provided the shirt's wicking effect. The anatomically cut top also included underarm and back mesh panels for ventilation. On the back appeared what looked like hundreds of dots but were actually tiny laser-cut holes in the shape of the Spurs crest. The underarm and side panels appeared to be formed by a grey chevron pattern but were actually mesh. This feature was only available on the players' match shirts.

The shirt also featured metallic silver tape across the shoulders and there was a single-button collar that, on the replica version, was branded 'Under Armour', and a metallic silver rectangle also appeared on the base of the placket.

The overall effect of the innovative shirt was aesthetically pleasing, but there were issues with the material's original composition. Initially the players did not like the flannel feel of the material, so it was altered to a different, lighter Heatgear composition after the second game of the season against West Brom, with the holes being replaced with grey dots. Under Armour's ambitious shirt design was accentuated by the equally bold decision to break with tradition and reintroduce white shorts to accompany it.

*Above: Gareth Bale was by now playing in the No.11 shirt*

*Above: The Investec 'cup' version of the shirt was worn in the Europa League and featured the new style UEFA 'Respect' badges*

# AWAY 2012/13

*Match worn by* MICHAEL DAWSON

Under Armour's smart navy away shirt included reinforced half cuffs and a shallow v-neck. Match worn examples are extremely rare because it was only worn during pre-season and in away games at Newcastle, Stoke, Swansea, Fulham and Sunderland. No Investec 'cup' version was ever worn

# THIRD 2012/13

*Match worn by* STEVEN CAULKER

This shirt was another ambitious Under Armour design. The yellow trim on the cuffs was made of flannel. On the long-sleeved version (far right), the crest is much lower than on the short-sleeved version. This was a response to a request from Gareth Bale who complained that the higher position meant the crest rubbed against and irritated his skin. This alteration only appeared on the long-sleeved shirt and, following Bale, other players then started to favour it over the short-sleeved version. The Aurasma version was worn seven times in the Premier League, while the Investec edition was worn just once, in the FA Cup fourth round against Leeds United

Note the lower club crest position on the long-sleeved Premier League version of the shirt

# HOME 2013/14

*Match worn by* CHRISTIAN ERIKSEN

Spurs took to the field for the 2013/14 season in a new Under Armour shirt notable for its unusual collar design and two brand-new sponsors.

Made from improved Heatgear fabric developed to a new composition, the shirt's retro-style collar was formed from an elasticated navy crew-neck with a central white stripe, with the two halves meeting in a v-shape to form a placket. The same navy and white band appeared on the cuffs of both the long and short-sleeved versions and, together with an uncluttered plain white body and sleeves, produced a clean design that certainly felt more traditionally Spurs than its predecessor.

In addition to the design changes, the shirt was given a whole new appearance thanks to the introduction of two new shirt sponsors. Hewlett-Packard were back as the main sponsor with a circular, electric blue logo. Now rebranded 'HP', the company had bought Autonomy and agreed to continue sponsoring the Premier League shirt for one more season. Insurance services provider AIA took over as cup sponsor, starting a long-standing relationship with the group which focuses much of its business in Asia, an increasingly important market for Premier League clubs.

The shirt also originally included the wording 'Under Armour' on each sleeve, but the text was deemed too large by the Premier League who requested it be made smaller. This was duly complied with by using the same size text that had already appeared on junior replica shirts.

The Premier League letters, numbers and sleeve badges were all produced in a new vinyl material called 'PS-Pro', produced by Sporting ID, which was more durable than the previous Lextra and SenCilla materials.

The departure of Gareth Bale to Real Madrid prompted a blitz of summer purchases before the 2013/14 season, with no fewer than seven new arrivals at White Hart Lane, the most successful being Danish international playmaker Christian Eriksen, who was signed from Ajax.

*Above: Christian Eriksen, who swiftly became a firm favourite amongst Spurs supporters, on the attack against Southampton at White Hart Lane*

*Above: A new name appeared on the 'cup' version of this shirt, but AIA would shortly become the club's main sponsor*

# AWAY 2013/14

*Match worn by* PAULINHO

The unfussy sky blue away shirt was only worn in the Premier League, with this battle-scarred Paulinho jersey having seen action against Sunderland in December. A number of AIA shirts were produced as an emergency European kit, but they were never worn

# THIRD 2013/14

*Match worn by* NACER CHADLI

A popular shirt amongst the supporters, the navy third jersey had a shallow v-neck collar trimmed in light blue and was only worn once competitively in Europe, against Tromso, with a smaller AIA sponsor logo to comply with UEFA regulations. The Under Armour wording on the sleeve was banned by UEFA, so the Spurs kit team cleverly used pieces of old flock European numbers cut into strips and heat-pressed on to the sleeves to cover the text. It was seen on one occasion with a full-sized AIA logo, when it was given an outing for Ledley King's testimonial

*The HP Premier League shirt was worn against Cardiff, Manchester City and Stoke*

# HOME 2014/15

*Match worn by* HARRY KANE

The three Under Armour shirts produced for the 2014/15 campaign were designed to honour Bill Nicholson, 10 years after the legendary Spurs manager had passed away.

The outcome was the 'Echoes of Glory' collection, in reference to one of Bill Nick's most famous quotes. "At Spurs we set our sights very high," the great man once said, "so that even failure will have in it an echo of glory".

The home shirt in the range acknowledged Tottenham's most successful manager in a subtle but intriguing way. The unusual collar design featured a yellow trim that broke up the navy bar across the chest and sleeves, symbolising the gates at the entrance to White Hart Lane on Bill Nicholson Way. The gates were immortalised in the famous photograph in which the Double-winning gaffer is pictured smiling and opening the entrance to his football kingdom.

The tribute to Bill Nick was continued with an elasticated stripe stitched on the inside of the collar on both the home and away shirts that read 'BN' and '11' in a circle – 11 being the number of trophies won while he was at the club as both a player and manager.

On players' shirts like this one worn by Harry Kane – the emerging new home-grown star who played in the finest of Tottenham traditions that Nicholson did so much to forge – there were laser-cut holes in a diamond panel under the arms for ventilation.

This was the season that the various multiple sponsor arrangement was dropped and AIA took over as the sole shirt sponsor for all competitions.

*Above: For the 2014/15 season the Premier League sleeve patches now came in vinyl*

*Left: Harry Kane on the ball in the club's third Under Armour home shirt, designed in honour of the great Bill Nicholson*

# AWAY 2014/15

*Match shirt of* HARRY KANE

*Black kits have always proven popular with Tottenham supporters and this one, with its distinctive yellow trim that cleverly paid tribute to the achievements of Bill Nicholson, was no exception. A shade of yellow was actually introduced as an alternative kit colour during Nicholson's tenure in 1958, while the central pinstripe detail has 11 stripes to represent Nicholson's trophy haul. The shirt was worn away to Manchester City, Swansea and QPR*

# THIRD 2014/15

*Match worn by* KYLE WALKER

The third shirt, in yellow and deep navy, featured three blocks of the 11 stripes motif on the sleeves and was actually worn more frequently than the designated away shirt, a total of nine times: against Stoke, Southampton, Newcastle, West Brom, Sheffield United, Sunderland and Leicester in domestic competition, and against Besiktas and Partizan Belgrade in Europe

# LEAGUE CUP FINAL 2015

*Match worn by* CHRISTIAN ERIKSEN

It was appropriate that Tottenham got to a major cup final wearing one of the Bill Nicholson tribute kits. And while the result did not go in Spurs' favour, with Chelsea winning 2-0, the performance showed that there was certainly a bright future ahead.

New manager Mauricio Pochettino was beginning to make his mark on the side, forging a young and vibrant team that within a year would be playing some of the best football seen from players in a Spurs shirt for decades.

A key figure in that progress was Christian Eriksen, who so nearly gave Spurs the lead at Wembley with a first-half free-kick that smacked off the crossbar. Eriksen's shirt from the final does not differ to any great extent from the normal home shirt for that season, save for the usual match-specific details and sponsor sleeve patches.

Between the Under Armour logo and the Spurs crest appeared the match detail 'CAPITAL ONE CUP FINAL', 'WEMBLEY STADIUM' and '1 MARCH 2015' over three lines. This wording was not embroidered but heat-applied plastic vinyl lettering. The last time a heat-applied process (rather than embroidery) was used for a Spurs shirt in a showpiece match was for the 1982 League Cup final, but on that occasion flock material was used instead of vinyl.

The sleeve patches featured the branding for the competition's new sponsor, Capital One, now in the third year of their deal with the Football League, whose own logo was integrated within the badge *(right)*.

The back of the shirt retained the large-style Premier League names and numbers in navy.

*Defeat to Chelsea in the 2015 Capital One Cup final was hard to take – especially as Christian Eriksen hit the crossbar in the first half*

# HOME 2015/16

*Match worn by* HEUNG-MIN SON

For the first time ever a Tottenham jersey sported a sash, and Under Armour's 2015/16 shirt was consequently nicknamed the 'Seatbelt Shirt'.

Officially described as a 'Heritage Sash', the diagonal navy embellishment ran from the right shoulder to the bottom left of the shirt's front and featured six lines inspired by the design of the shield that sat beneath the golden cockerel statue on the top of White Hart Lane's East Stand. Navy was also added to the wrapover v-neck and the cuffs, both unusually trimmed with grey.

Another new detail – a redesigned Europa League badge featuring a stylised rendering of the competition's trophy – made its debut for the 2015/16 campaign and was applied to the right sleeve for European matches. The updated UEFA 'Respect' badge, in the same flock material, was placed on the left.

In another sign of the growing use of branding for competitions and sponsors on football shirts, this was the first season that it was compulsory for teams to wear Emirates sleeve badges during FA Cup matches to name-check the competition's new sponsor. The requirement was not universally applied – non-league teams were given discretionary exemption, except when playing in live televised games – but all teams who joined the famous competition from the third round onwards were obliged to wear them.

Heung-Min Son, a £22 million capture from Bayer Leverkusen, wore this shirt for the home Europa League group stage tie against Qarabag in September 2015 – a match in which the dynamic South Korean scored twice in a 3-1 win.

*Above: Heung-Min Son in action against Qarabag FK, with his shirt sporting a new design of the Europa League badge (above, right)*

*Right: From 2015/16, FA Cup shirts carried competition logos, including branding for new sponsors Emirates*

# AWAY 2015/16

*Match worn by* DELE ALLI

*Broad navy bands to the front of this light blue shirt gave it a very anatomical look, mimicking the pattern of chest and abdomen muscles. It was only worn five times: in the Europa League against Monaco, as pictured here, and away at Swansea, Southampton, Stoke and Newcastle*

# THIRD 2015/16

*Match worn by* TOBY ALDERWEIRELD

Six stripes appeared
again on the purple third
shirt, this time as part of a
thick elasticated cuff that
accentuated the size of the
wearer's biceps. The grey
trim that was seen on the
home shirt was repeated
on the back of the hem and
in a shallow non-wrapover
v-neck. This shirt was
only worn twice, against
Sunderland and West Brom.
The player versions came up
slightly big so the players
tended to drop a size for
match wear

# HOME 2016/17

*Match worn by* DANNY ROSE

Under Armour's final season as Tottenham's kit supplier turned out to be something special. Not only was it worn during a spectacular league campaign but it also saw action in the Champions League in which the club appeared for the first time since the 2010/11 season, and the design was very much a nod to the shirt worn by Gareth Bale and co. during that memorable adventure.

The most noteworthy distinguishing feature on Under Armour's fourth and final home shirt was a thick navy band across the shoulders which was interrupted only by an unusual collar arrangement which featured gold trim. This colour was repeated on the cuffs.

It was a shirt that was popular with the fans, and for good reason given its associations with such an outstanding Spurs side. Mauricio Pochettino's third season in charge saw Tottenham's most concerted challenge for the league title since the 1960s. The Argentinian's increasingly potent team had gone close the season before when they finished third, but in 2016/17 Spurs were the only side to consistently challenge Chelsea. In the end Spurs finished a gallant second, achieving a club-record 86 points, a tally that would have been enough to win the Premier League title in eight of the previous seasons of the competition. Spurs were unbeaten at home throughout the league season and were the team that scored the most goals and conceded the fewest, resulting in an astonishing goal difference of plus 60.

A decade after its last revamp, the Premier League branding on the shirts of all member clubs was updated, and new circular sleeve badges were introduced. These reverted back to flock material, replacing the previous vinyl, but for this season the old-style universal letter and number font remained.

This particular shirt, complete with bloodstain, was worn by all-action full-back Danny Rose in the magnificent 2-0 home victory over Chelsea.

*Above: Danny Rose powers forward in the club's final Under Armour shirt, which included the new Premier League sleeve badges*

*Right: The European version of this shirt carried the club's own style of name and numbers*

# AWAY 2016/17

*Match worn by* ERIC DIER

The smart-looking navy
away shirt with gold-
trimmed crew-neck and thick
cuffs was surprisingly only
worn twice: in the Champions
League against Monaco
– when it incorporated
the competition's starball
logo (far right) – and in the
Premier League against
Stoke City

# THIRD 2016/17

*Match worn by* VICTOR WANYAMA

Gold was used as the main colour on a Spurs shirt for the first time since Bill Nicholson experimented with it for floodlit matches back in 1958. The effect was completed with pinstripes, this time in navy, which have often proved popular with Spurs fans. The jersey was worn just seven times: against Middlesbrough, West Brom, Southampton, Sunderland, Swansea and Leicester in the league, and against Fulham in the FA Cup

# THE LANE: THE FINALE 2017

*Match worn by* DELE ALLI

Under Armour's final act in its role as Spurs kit supplier was to produce a one-off shirt to commemorate a momentous occasion – the final game at the original White Hart Lane.

All season Tottenham had been playing their home games next to the futuristic superstructure that was rising out of the ground behind the North Stand, and by the final weeks of the season the concrete and steel that would soon become the club's state-of-the-art new home was starting to dwarf the existing stadium. Then, on an intensely emotional day on 14 May 2017 the club and its supporters bade a tearful yet joyful farewell to the old White Hart Lane and a pitch that had stood on the same plot of land for the last 118 years.

Premier League rules required all clubs' colours and kit designs to be registered at the start of the season and retained throughout, so producing a completely bespoke shirt for this one match was not an option for Under Armour's designers.

The authorities did, however, give permission for Tottenham to add commemorative match details in heat-pressed letters spread over four lines. These read 'TOTTENHAM HOTSPUR vs MANCHESTER UNITED, 14 MAY 2017' and were centrally positioned between the crest and the Under Armour logo. In addition, the AIA sponsor logo had to be reduced to the smaller 'European' size in order to allow room for another special feature: the logo of the Tottenham Tribute Trust – the charity set up to look after former Spurs players – appearing under the 'I' of AIA.

After the match, a passionate and convincing 2-1 win over United that did justice to the occasion, the players' shirts were auctioned off in aid of the Tottenham Tribute Trust. The final prices achieved stunning valuations, including almost £10,000 for Harry Kane's shirt.

Match worn shirts from the final match at White Hart Lane are totally unique and, therefore, understandably highly collectable.

*Above: Dele Alli in action during the emotional final match at White Hart Lane*

*Above: On the reverse, above each player's name and number, was the stylish 'The Lane Finale' logo which incorporated the club crest in gold, flanked by the dates '1899' and '2017', above a blue shield, with the wording 'The Lane', which replicated the design of the shield that had proudly adorned the East Stand for decades*

TOTTENHAM HOTSPUR
VS
MANCHESTER UNITED
14 MAY 2017

# THE LANE: THE FINALE 2017

*Tracksuit and warm-up t-shirt of DELE ALLI*

*Above and right: Before the match the players warmed up in 'Tottenham Tribute Trust' t-shirts*

Above and left: The Spurs players ran out for the last-ever game at White Hart Lane in smart, one-off tracksuit tops complete with match detail embroidery

# THE ONES THAT GOT AWAY

The challenge of putting together a complete collection of Tottenham Hotspur player shirts for inclusion in this book has required a great deal of effort and research, but ultimately it is an impossible task.

The further you go back in the club's history, naturally there are fewer jerseys in existence. None of the weird and wonderful Victorian-era variations of the Spurs shirt have survived. No one appears to have saved a jersey from the 1901 FA Cup triumph or the 1921 final, even though the whereabouts of at least one worn by opponents Wolverhampton Wanderers is known. In fact even the most comprehensive search has turned up nothing lilywhite, or indeed of any other hue, from before the Second World War. There was simply no concept in those days that football match shirts would one day become highly treasured historical artefacts.

## MISSING SHIRTS

The search for Spurs shirts going back 50 years has proven slightly more fruitful, although the various styles of alternative or change jerseys have proved the most elusive.

The first of these missing shirts from the modern era is the classic crew-necked navy blue away jersey. First introduced in 1962 with the old-style, Double-winning cockerel crest within a white shield (changed in 1967, in line with the home shirt, to include the new-style cockerel-on-ball crest embroidered in white), in keeping with the fashion of the time this jersey had long sleeves along with a white crew-neck and cuffs and has subsequently become a hugely popular retro replica jersey. One of the reasons that no known examples of this style have surfaced, despite extensive searching, is that it was never worn in a major cup final, and from this era it is generally only such jerseys that ever found their way out of the White Hart Lane kit room.

Equally rare and for the same reason is the club's first-ever yellow away shirt, introduced in 1969 after the Football League deemed that navy blue was too close to the black of the match officials' uniforms. Following discussions between Bill Nicholson and outfitters, Ron Goodman Sports, who were Umbro's official distributors to the club, yellow was chosen because it was the colour that clashed with the fewest number of opposition teams' home shirts. Spurs introduced a yellow long-sleeved Umbro 'Self Association Trim' Aztec jersey, with the trim unusually being a white crew-neck and cuffs, with a navy club crest and white numbers. Worn with navy shorts, other than on one occasion against Derby when white shorts were worn, this kit was changed after just two seasons – an unusually short lifespan for the era – and replaced with a solid yellow reverse of the home shirt, with royal blue numbers. Incidentally, Spurs were one of a small number of clubs who switched to yellow away shirts before Brazil made it fashionable after the 1970 World Cup.

*Below, left: Frank Saul models the popular navy away shirt worn during the 1961 Double season*

*Below, right: Joe Kinnear in the rare yellow away shirt with white collar and cuffs. There are no known examples of this shirt in existence*

In the early 1970s, Umbro and other manufacturers were now experimenting with man-made fabrics including a material called Bri-Nylon. The idea was that these were lighter, easier to wash and more durable than cotton. But they were extremely coarse and many players found them uncomfortable. Steve Perryman says: "I have no memory of a Spurs team wearing these shirts." However, in the pre- and early part of the 1972 and 1973 seasons, Bill Nicholson did trial a new material designed with player comfort in mind.

Since the late 1800s a company called the Cellular Clothing Company had produced a perforated, or aerated, material branded 'Aertex', which they used predominantly to produce underwear. By the mid-1960s Umbro had developed this material in to what is considered to be the first modern sports performance fabric and used it to

## NO EXAMPLES OF THE CREW-NECKED NAVY 1960S AWAY SHIRTS HAVE SURFACED

create football shirts and shorts, branded 'Airtex' rather than 'Aertex', designed for use in warm or humid conditions. The material was made famous when Umbro provided Airtex shirts for the England team (and others, including West Germany) to wear at the Mexico 1970 World Cup. The shirts were lighter than their standard cotton counterparts with ventilation provided by the perforations.

*Considered an all-time classic, sadly there are no known examples of the long-sleeved, crew-necked navy away shirt worn between 1962–67 – seen here in action against Fulham in October 1966*

*Central defender Mike Dillon only played 29 matches for Spurs but at least one of them, in September 1973, was in the extremely rare Airtex home jersey*

## THE AIRTEX SPURS SHIRT IS POSSIBLY THE RAREST OF THE MODERN ERA

Nicholson was one of the earliest managers to understand the correlation between player comfort and performance. In 1972 he ordered the first set of Airtex shirts for Spurs although these were in short sleeves to be worn on warm days at the start of the season or if the club was on tour in a hot country. As Perryman recalls: "I remember England wore them at the 1970 World Cup and I'd worn them for the Under-23s. Bill covered everything so it was only natural that we should at some stage try them".

Airtex versions of the home shirt were used eight times at the start of the 1972/73 season – the club never wore an Airtex away shirt – and then again in the early stages of the 1973/74 season. Unfortunately, because they were more lightweight than their full-cotton counterparts, they were not as robust. As Perryman remembers: "The shirts looked and felt great when we first wore them, but washing significantly affected the shape". This may be the reason why Bill Nick did not continue with the experiment so no further shirts were ordered and consequently none have survived. This makes it quite possibly the rarest Spurs shirt of the modern era.

However, in a twist to the tale, Tony Parks remembers being in the kit room when he was an apprentice and seeing Johnny Wallis take an Airtex home shirt featuring embroidery for the 1973 League Cup final from a box.

"I remember seeing this beautiful, fully embroidered Airtex shirt and asking Wal what it was," remembers Parks. "He showed me the 1973 FL CUP FINAL embroidery and I asked if I could have it. He said, 'No way you're not having one of my shirts', of course, and stuffed it back in the box."

It would appear that at least one set of fully embroidered short-sleeved Airtex shirts was produced for the final, but in the end the standard long-sleeved jerseys were selected for the match. Very few people knew of the existence of these shirts, they never saw the light of day and what became of them remains a mystery to this day.

There are several examples over the years of Spurs shirt styles that were worn for just a handful of games, but

After the World Cup, Umbro's Airtex shirts became fashionable in the Football League, and many teams began wearing them although – unlike the England 1970 World Cup shirts – quite often in long sleeves. Only ever available to professional clubs, they never appeared in the company's standard teamwear 'Umbrochure' catalogue due to the expense of manufacture.

with the exception of those worn for cup finals there are few where it can be categorically stated that they were only worn once by the first team. However, on 19 February 1977 Tottenham played away at Leeds United wearing an unfamiliar all-royal blue strip without a club crest. The choice stemmed again from the view of the football authorities that white (Leeds' home colours) and yellow (Spurs' away shirt colour) constituted a clash. Sourced as an emergency one-off, given the lack of a club crest even if such a shirt did surface today it would be extremely hard to verify that it had actually been worn at Elland Road. However, evidence of how shirts were handed down through the club is the fact that this blue kit was used at least once by the Spurs youth team, in an FA Youth Cup semi-final match away to Crystal Palace in April 1977.

From the late 1970s and into the early 1980s, commercialism in the form of sponsorship and branding came into the game and resulted in far more kit styles and variations, of which many more examples have survived – partly because Spurs were successful and reached a number of memorable cup finals during the period. However, with so many subtle changes to shirts for different reasons, inevitably there are some absentees from *The Spurs Shirt* collection .

Spurs were actually one of the last of the major English clubs to feature sponsorship on their shirts. But they did dip their toe into the water with a deal with stationary company Everard Ovenden whose 'EO Papers' logo featured on the back of the players' warm-up tracksuits for the 1980/81 season.

The first ever Spurs shirt to feature a sponsor appeared at the end of that season, but the logo was not – as many Spurs supporters might think – the name of beer brand Holsten. We know from grainy photographs from a post-season tour to Istanbul in the summer of 1981 that the first-ever logo to be emblazoned across the chest of the famous Spurs jersey was in fact Sultan Hali – an established carpet, rug and soft furnishings retailer in the Turkish capital. At the time Spurs were resistant to having a sponsor on the sacred lilywhite shirt for domestic

competition, however they were open to the idea on foreign tours which would receive minimal coverage back home. There are no known surviving examples of this unique and historic shirt, which we know from photographs was worn against Trabzonspor and it is also believed to have been worn against Fenerbahce.

The end of season tours to Swaziland of 1983 and 1984 threw up some further fascinating variations of the Spurs shirt. The first African adventure witnessed one of the strangest and indeed unlikely football shirts a Spurs

*Above: In February 1977 Neil McNab and his Spurs teammates played Leeds at Elland Road in an unusual all-royal blue kit with no club crest*

*Left: The Spurs players line-up with their shirts carrying a sponsorship logo for the first time, against Trabzonspor of Turkey in the summer of 1981*

*Far left: The unlikely first sponsor to appear on the Spurs kit was EO Papers in 1980*

*Above: Perhaps the strangest Spurs shirt of them all was the joint Tottenham Hotspur/Manchester United jersey worn on tour to Swaziland in 1983*

*Right: Two extremely rare shirts from African tours in the 1980s. The SWAZI SPA shirt comes from the collection of Garth Crooks, although it is not known exactly when it was worn*

player has ever worn – a combined Tottenham Hotspur/Manchester United jersey. Only a handful of poor quality photographs exist from a game in which five Spurs outfield players and five from United combined to form a team labelled 'Spur United' to take on the Swaziland national team, and they appear to show the touring players in white Le Coq Sportif shirts with red trim which feature the club crests of both English clubs. Though not strictly a Tottenham Hotspur jersey, with no surviving examples known this almost unbelievable anomaly would appear to be lost and, to many, probably best forgotten!

One more obscure Swaziland-related shirt that has found its way on to these pages is the jersey from the summer 1984 tour, where Spurs played two matches, this time against Liverpool in the south-east African country. On this occasion the club's standard Le Coq Sportif home shirts carried the logo of Black Cat, a South African brand of peanut butter.

It wasn't until December 1983 that Holsten first appeared on the Spurs shirt, a fact which could easily confuse anyone who stumbled upon a 1980–82 yellow Le Coq Sportif away jersey – the style with the blue epaulettes as worn in the 1982 FA Cup final – with a Holsten logo on the front. The reason for this apparent chronological anomaly

## FOREIGN TOURS IN THE 1980S THREW UP SOME FASCINATING VARIATIONS OF THE SPURS SHIRT

is that the shirt – almost two years after the end of its lifespan – was brought out of retirement, with Holsten logo added, for two matches in April 1984, both times against teams whose blue and white colours clashed with both Tottenham's white home and powder blue away shirts. The first match was the UEFA Cup semi-final first leg away to Hajduk Split on 11 April 1984, for which the smaller European competition Holsten logo was embroidered on to old stock of this first Le Coq Sportif away shirt. And then the same jerseys were used later the same month for the visit to QPR. It is safe to say that this variation is extremely rare and although no examples could be found for inclusion in this book, if any were to exist it is likely they would be in the collections of any Croatian players who swapped after the match in Split.

As we have seen with the visits to Turkey and Swaziland, foreign tours have tended to throw up all sorts of sponsor variations and oddities. There have also been examples of the first team shirts used on tours being devoid of a sponsor's logo altogether. At the post-season Kirin Cup in Japan in 1991, the title sponsor of the mini-tournament was a Japanese beer company, which caused a conflict, and is why the new-style Umbro shirts were used but without their usual Holsten logo. But it was a surprise to see Holsten across the chest of the shirts worn in the five games played in Norway during the pre-seasons of 1991 and 1993, a country where alcoholic sponsorship had been banned since 1975.

In the space of two months in 2005, two more unfamiliar sponsored shirts were worn by Spurs on foreign tours. Firstly, for an end of season visit to Mauritius in May when they played against Club M, the team shirts carried the

brand of travel agents and tour sponsors Imbel Travel. Two months later, in July, the club took part in the Peace Cup, a pre-season tournament in South Korea where a special one-off sponsorship agreement was arranged with financial services company Standard Charter.

As much as these different sponsored tour shirts are sought after and desirable to keen collectors, their rarity does not necessarily make them valuable.

*Far left: Spurs take on Hajduk Split in the UEFA Cup in 1984 wearing a set of 1980–82 away shirts with Holsten logos added*

*Left: An Imbel Travel-sponsored jersey worn on an end of season tour to Mauritius in 2005*

*Left, below: In July 2005 Spurs played in the Peace Cup in South Korea in their new Kappa jerseys with Standard Chartered on the front*

*Right: Whilst there have been numerous testimonial matches over the course of the club's history, Spurs match shirts have only included bespoke match details to mark the occasion three times– including this 1997 match against Fiorentina in honour of midfielder David Howells*

*Facing page, left: Shirts from two of the three occasions when shirts worn during a testimonial match for a Spurs player have included match details – David Howells' match against Fiorentina in 1997 (top) and Justin Edinburgh's game against Portsmouth in 2000 (below)*

*Facing page, right: Two examples of shirts from the annual charity match when the club auctions off the match shirts to raise money for the designated cause. The top shirt is from the 2011/12 match against Manchester United, the first of such occasions which was in aid of the Tottenham Foundation. In 2013/14 Spurs played Fulham in aid of no less than six charities (below)*

## ONE-OFFS

In addition to missing and very rare examples, there is another group of Spurs shirts that come under the heading of one-offs; in other words shirts that for some reason are unique to a single game. There have been a number of one-off celebratory games for long service to the football club, when players, a couple of managers and even the kit men have been awarded a benefit match. From Jimmy Greaves in the 1970s, through to Steve Perryman and Glenn Hoddle in the '80s, to Gary Mabbutt in the 1990s, Tottenham Hotspur have rewarded a number of loyal servants by holding a testimonial game in their honour. But even though these are unique one-off games, only three players from the last 20 odd years have worn shirts marking the occasion with commemorative match detail: David Howells in 1997, when the Spurs team wore an away shirt against Fiorentina, Justin Edinburgh in May 2000, when Portsmouth were the opposition, and then Ledley King's memorable occasion in May 2014 which saw a Spurs XI take on a Ledley Guest XI, and the two teams donned Tottenham Hotspur home and away shirts respectively.

A set of shirts that fits into this group are the now annual poppy shirts, featured elsewhere in this book, and also the shirts produced for the club's once-a-season charity game. This tradition, started in 2011/12 with the Tottenham Foundation, sees space on the shirt for a home match given over to a charity organisation. After the match the shirts are auctioned, with thousands of pounds raised every year for a different worthy cause.

There was also a set of one-off shirts produced for the final game at White Hart Lane in May 2017 – The Finale – which is featured elsewhere in *The Spurs Shirt*.

One final example of the Spurs shirt used only for a single game, and another in the non-sponsored oddity jersey category, is the one that the team wore for a pre-season friendly away to Bournemouth in 2010. These were in fact training shirts, worn because the late signing of the new Autonomy sponsorship deal meant that the shirts for the upcoming campaign were not yet fully prepared.

## KIT-SHARING

There have been a handful of occasions when, for a variety of reasons, Spurs have worn another team's shirts for a match, or the opposition have turned out in a Tottenham Hotspur kit.

The first example of the latter was in 1956 when the touring Racing Club de Paris team played a friendly at White Hart Lane and, according to former player Tommy Harmer, "turned up without any playing kit". Racing ended up playing the match in a set of Spurs' 1949–52 solid navy blue away shirts. The strip was actually the first Sours Rayon kit, and this is actually the first-ever occasion when the team wore white shorts with their white shirts. It appears to have been very much pre-planned, as Spurs are listed in the match programme as wearing all-white. Racing were listed in programme as playing in their standard home colours of sky blue and white, and rather than the French team

## THERE ARE SOME SPURS SHIRTS THAT FOR SOME REASON OR ANOTHER ARE UNIQUE TO A SINGLE GAME

*Seven examples of Spurs
youth team shirts from
Hummel, Umbro and adidas
which varied from those
worn by the first team*

kit upon opponents Manchester City. In August 1985, with bright August sunshine and Spurs in their home strip, the referee deemed that there wasn't enough of a contrast with City's sky blue shirts and the hosts switched to their red-and-black-striped away jerseys. And there was a similar issue at Maine Road in December 1990 when fog at a televised game meant that City were again ordered to change in to their maroon away shirts to create enough of a contrast to Spurs' now yellow away strip.

## THE INNOCENCE OF YOUTH

Another group of rare and unusual Spurs shirts that often raise eyebrows are variations produced specifically for the youth teams.

During the first period when beer brand Holsten was the club's shirt sponsor, in the Le Coq Sportif years from 1984 to 1985, the youth team shirts carried the Holsten logos whilst replica shirts in child and youth sizes – sold in the club shop – did not. But when Hummel took over as kit manufacturers in 1985, the decision was taken not to include their main sponsor's logo on the shirts of the club's youth teams as it was deemed inappropriate and as a result the shirts carried no sponsor branding at all. Conversely, the child-size replica Hummel shirts did include Holsten logos.

Perhaps as a result of the mix-up with the unsponsored youth team shirts at the 1987 FA Cup final, from the 1988/89 season onwards the club's junior teams played in shirts emblazoned with 'Hummel' in unusual outline lettering across the chest. Umbro followed suit when they took over from Hummel in 1991, and changed the policy back to removing the alcoholic sponsor from child-size replicas. Somehow a Spurs shirt with 'Umbro' rather than 'Holsten' across the front ended up being worn by Gazza when, having played for Lazio in the second leg of the Umbro-sponsored Capital Cup against Spurs, he lifted the trophy after the match.

In 1993, until 1995, computer games company SEGA replaced Umbro as the youth team shirt sponsor until Umbro and Holsten were replaced by Pony and Hewlett-Packard in 1995 and, as it was not an age-appropriate brand, the HP logo appeared on youth team shirts. When Holsten returned as the main shirt sponsor during the adidas era, the youth team reverted back to being blank without any sponsorship logo.

*Above: Neil Ruddock is pictured in an unsponsored Hummel youth team shirt in 1985*

*Left: Gazza lifts the so-called Capital Cup following a glorified friendly against Lazio in 1991 in an Umbro-sponsored Spurs shirt having played against Spurs for his new Italian employers*

forgetting their kit as Harmer suggested it is more likely that on arrival at the ground this strip was deemed too close to Spurs' all-white for a match under floodlights.

A similar thing happened in the UEFA Cup in 1972 when Norwegian side Lyn Oslo played the second leg of their tie against Spurs in the home team's yellow away strip – presumably because the referee deemed that the Norwegians' red and white shirts clashed with Tottenham Hotspur's white.

The roles were reversed for Spurs when they travelled to Highfield Road, then home of Coventry City, in December 1986. After arriving with only their alternative navy away kit, Tottenham Hotspur were ordered to play in Coventry's yellow away shirts, as the referee deemed their colours too close to City's blue and white stripes.

There were also two occasions during the club's Hummel era when the weather conditions enforced a change of

# WATCH US RISE
## 2017–

NIKE

# WATCH US RISE

With Tottenham Hotspur Football Club entering a bright new era – both off the pitch with the incredible new stadium taking shape and on it where top four Premier League finishes and Champions League qualification were becoming the norm rather than the exception – the signing of a multi-year partnership with global giants Nike provided another indication that Spurs were now firmly established back amongst the elite of English football.

In June 2017 the club announced that they would run out at Wembley in their first Nike kit, and then when the new stadium back in N17 was completed the Tottenham Experience, developed in collaboration with Nike, would provide a retail experience to rival any sporting organisation in the world.

"We are delighted to be partnering with Nike, one of the world's leading brands," enthused chairman Daniel Levy. "Nike is committed to partnering with us both at home, at a time when our new stadium scheme is the catalyst for the regeneration of Tottenham, and globally, with our growing fan base mirrored by Nike's worldwide reach."

Working closely with Spurs, Nike's team delved deep into Tottenham's history for inspiration for its first set of kits and combined it with a modern approach to kit design.

"Everyone is aware of the history and tradition of Spurs," explained the company's Global Football Apparel Product Line Manager, Matthew Shotton. "With a club like Spurs we have to respect those traditions. Tottenham's values run so deep. We had initial meetings with the marketing team, and we were taken through their brand positioning and insights to understand how deep those roots are; the individuals who have been associated with the club, right through the core of the club from the players and management to the fans.

"But it's not a club stuck in the past. There is a genuine excitement with everything going on and about

*Far left: The Nike era began in style with a smart and classically Spurs home kit for 2017/18*

*Above: The popular navy away shirt was designed to look good on both players and fans alike*

*Below: The 1960s club crest in a shield (left) which was mirrored on the 2017/18 version (right)*

## THE NEW KITS CAPTURED THE SPURS STYLE WITH THE MODERN AND DYNAMIC NIKE LOOK AND FEEL

what the future may hold. This is potentially one of the most exciting times the club has ever had. We have tried to create kits that align with that – we wanted to stay true to their iconic identity but also allow the innovation to show through."

Consequently, the resulting set of home and away kits – which were universally well-received – captured the Spurs style as well as the modern and dynamic look and feel with which Nike is synonymous.

"For the first season we really wanted to reference the iconic identity that Spurs have – the pure elegance of the lilywhite kit stripped back to its purest form," Shotton said. "That was the starting point. We wanted to be respectful and package that identity for the team to take to Wembley."

The latter objective was primarily achieved through the redesigned crest for the campaign, which saw the cockerel-on-ball emblem encased in a shield reminiscent of that worn during the glory glory years of the early '60s.

"When Spurs won the Double in 1960/61, the crowning moment came at Wembley. We wanted to tie that together and bring the shield identity back around the crest," explained Shotton. "It was a true nod to that glorious moment in the past but also very much a nod to the current crop of players with the potential to make history for themselves. It was aligning with the past but in a very modern way. It's a partnership with Spurs: as a brand we saw there was an opportunity and a real excitement to work with a club with such a hugely rich history and such a storied tradition."

But whilst the home and away shirts definitely carried a traditional look and feel, the technology behind them was very much from the present. This innovation came in the form of the 'AeroSwift' technology used to create the shirts' fabric, based on exhaustive research and testing with professional players. Essentially the AeroSwift fabric is a recycled polyester material that enables the manufacturer

to knit in structured breathable areas – or 'open-holed technology' – in the shirt where it is most needed.

"What we do as a brand from a performance perspective is to solve issues players have on the pitch," said Shotton. "What we consistently get back from them is that when the shirt gets heavy through moisture, they become uncomfortable. Our benchmark is zero distraction – we don't want players noticing the shirt during the game. The knit structures that are visible in the shirt allow increased breathability and moisture management through wicking. So the shirt dries much quicker than in the past and the players are able to stay comfortable throughout the 90 minutes."

It all requires a manufacturer like Nike to strike a careful balance between how a shirt looks and what it does for the player. "We are a performance company and we'll always strive to provide innovative products to players that aid performance even just one per cent – that's what

we're always looking to do, to move forward and progress," Shotton said. "Aesthetics are very important. We want to be very respectful about the teams we work with. Football is a game of traditions and while we are a forward-thinking company we are very respectful of heritage. We knew that in the first year of partnership we wanted to make sure that what we did was faithful to those Tottenham characteristics.

"The synergy is perfect," Shotton adds. "It's the perfect time to establish that relationship and work together."

So, when Tottenham stepped out for their first home league game at Wembley in August 2017, it was in a shirt that was definably Spurs. It passed Nike's internal test – that if the crest is removed it is still recognisably a Tottenham jersey. In tandem with the classic navy away and the more daring, and indeed dazzling, purple and luminous yellow 'dazzle camo' third shirt, it got the Spurs-Nike relationship off to a flying and widely commended start.

# HOME 2017/18

*Match worn by* MOUSA DEMBELE

The 2017/18 campaign heralded the beginning of a brand-new multi-season kit partnership, with global American apparel giants Nike becoming the 11th manufacturer to be entrusted with the Spurs shirt.

Clean and stylish, Nike's first home shirt was classically Spurs and an instant hit with players and supporters alike. The pure and simple lilywhite was subtly embellished with three-quarter-length navy ventilation stripes down each side, and a neat two-stripe navy trim around three-quarters of the crew-neck collar with the word 'Spurs' neatly woven into the back of the neck.

The new shirt may have had an outwardly traditional look, but the technology behind Nike's 'Vapor' kit range – featuring AeroSwift technology, the company's most advanced performance fabric to date – was at the cutting edge. Designed in collaboration with top professional players to create football shirts that were cooler, more breathable and more comfortable than ever before, the Vapor jersey also provided what Nike's creative director Martin Lotti described as "a superhero aesthetic".

With Spurs playing all their home games at Wembley whilst the club's new stadium was being built back in N17, for one season only the famous cockerel proudly standing on a ball crest appeared on the left breast encased in a retro-style shield as a nod to that worn by Bill Nicholson's famous side which sealed their historic Double at the original stadium when they beat Leicester in the 1961 FA Cup final.

During the course of the season it was also seen with the Champions League starball and Emirates FA Cup sleeve patches (but still using the club's own font names and numbers), and for the first time League Cup sleeve patches with the logo of the competition's new sponsor, Carabao.

Worn with equally classic-looking navy shorts domestically and white shorts as per tradition in Europe, the new strip provided a perfect start to Spurs' new partnership with Nike.

*Above and right: The unwashed shirt featured here was worn by midfielder Mousa Dembele in the first 'home' game of the season against Chelsea*

*Top right: This shirt features the brand-new style of Premier League names and numbers, which included the rebranded Premier League logo for the first time*

# AWAY 2017/18

*Match worn by* JAN VERTONGHEN

*Oozing style, Nike's first Tottenham Hotspur away shirt was the exact 'reverse' of its home counterpart. The club's away jersey for domestic competition – the shirt featured here was worn by Jan Vertonghen in the first game of the season away to Newcastle – this style was primarily worn with navy shorts and socks although, when required, it was interchangeable with white shorts and socks which meant all versions of the strip were instantly identifiable as classic Spurs*

# THIRD 2017/18

*Match worn by* DAVINSON SANCHEZ

Whilst Nike's first home and away Spurs shirts were classically Tottenham, the third jersey was an altogether different proposition. Featuring a 'dazzle camo' design in dark purple with a bright yellow stripe on the arm, this shirt was registered as the first-choice away shirt for the UEFA Champions League. It was worn just twice, away to Real Madrid in the group stages (when the shirt featured here was worn by Davinson Sanchez) and then against Juventus in the quarter-final

# HOME 2018/19

*Match shirt of* HARRY KANE

Nike's '2018/19 Club Kit Collection' – featuring three innovative designs for the new home, away and third shirts – was, according to the manufacturer, designed to "skilfully balance Tottenham Hotspur's modern identity with its rich history" as the club prepared for the start of a new era in its stunning new home.

The home shirt – with its gradual blue fade coming up from the hem and smart navy collar – pays homage to the club's move into the stunning new Tottenham Hotspur Stadium, as well as conveying the vibrant characteristics of the club's dynamic young team.

According to Nike the jersey, along with blue shorts and blue and white socks also featuring a blue fade from the top "is intended to subtly reference the architecture of the new stadium while creating a dynamic head-to-toe gradient that reinforces the underlying explosive energy of the club's players, implying both speed and power".

The shirt undeniably adds an ultra-modern twist to the classic lilywhite and blue, with the 'VaporKnit' jersey featuring an ultra-light 'quick-dry' construction which, being significantly lighter than the previous season's jersey, lets players move freely at speed, as well as incorporating 'Nike Fast Fit' which 'delivers a locked-in feel where players need it most'.

To cement the connection with both Spurs' rich heritage and exciting future, the 2018/19 home shirt also features an 'inner pride message' on the inside collar – the postcode and coordinates of the centre circle at the club's former home, White Hart Lane, the site of which has now been overlapped by their magnificent new stadium.

*Right: Harry Kane in action in the 2018/19 shirt with its distinctive gradual fade*

*Right: The club crest on the shirt reverted to a stand-alone cockerel-on-ball motif without a surrounding shield*

# AWAY 2018/19

*Match shirt of* HARRY KANE

*Designed for use in the Premier League, the 2018/19 Nike away shirt incorporates two of the club's classic away shirt colours – dark and light blue – but injected with a lightning bolt of Nike energy and modernism. Constructed in what the manufacturer called "binary blue with polarised blue knit sleeves", the inside collar of the away jersey featured the message '#COYS' in reference to the commonly used social media hashtag abbreviation of 'Come on You Spurs'*

# THIRD 2018/19

*Match worn by* CHRISTIAN ERIKSEN

Continuing Nike's trend for conceptual third kits, this innovative shirt incorporates a map of Tottenham and pays homage to the club's roots in London N17. The first-ever primarily green Spurs away shirt, the colour choice was inspired by the logo of Charrington's Brewery, the company which originally owned the land where White Hart Lane was built. Intended primarily as an alternative Champions League and domestic cup jersey, it was actually used in the first away Premier League match of the season against Newcastle United

# THE COMPLETE HISTORY

*A comprehensive historical record of the Tottenham Hotspur Football Club kit, including change colours and variations, from 1883 to 2019*

1883/84 Home
1883/84 Home (Alt)
1883/84 Home (Alt)
1884/85 Home
1885/86 Home
1889/90 Home
1890–Oct 1895 Home
1895–98 Home
1898–1906 Home
1899–1903 2nd

1900/01 2nd (Alt)
1903–13 Home
1903/04 2nd
1904/05 2nd
1908 2nd
1908–12 2nd
1911–13 & 1915–19 Home
1912–14 Home (Alt)
1912–15 Home
1912–14 2nd

1919/20 Home
1920/21 Home
1920/21 2nd
1920/21 2nd (Alt)
1921–30 Home
1920–24 2nd
1921/22 2nd (Cup)
1925/26 2nd
1927–34 2nd
1930–Jan 1931 & 1933 Home

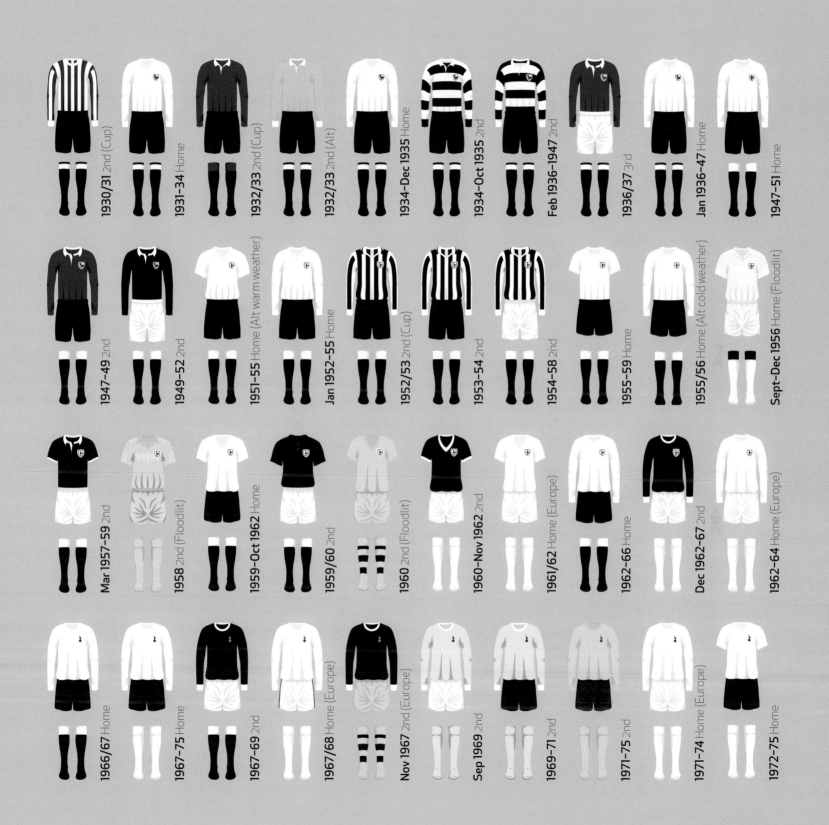

1930/31 2nd (Cup)

1931–34 Home

1932/33 2nd (Cup)

1932/33 2nd (Alt)

1934–Dec 1935 Home

1934–Oct 1935 2nd

Feb 1936–1947 2nd

1936/37 3rd

Jan 1936–47 Home

1947–51 Home

1947–49 2nd

1949–52 2nd

1951–55 Home (Alt warm weather)

Jan 1952–55 Home

1952/53 2nd (Cup)

1953–54 2nd

1954–58 2nd

1955–59 Home

1955/56 Home (Alt cold weather)

Sept–Dec 1956 Home (Floodlit)

Mar 1957–59 2nd

1958 2nd (Floodlit)

1959–Oct 1962 Home

1959/60 2nd

1960 2nd (Floodlit)

1960–Nov 1962 2nd

1961/62 Home (Europe)

1962–66 Home

Dec 1962–67 2nd

1962–64 Home (Europe)

1966/67 Home

1967–75 Home

1967–69 2nd

1967/68 Home (Europe)

Nov 1967 2nd (Europe)

Sep 1969 2nd

1969–71 2nd

1971–75 2nd

1971–74 Home (Europe)

1972–75 Home

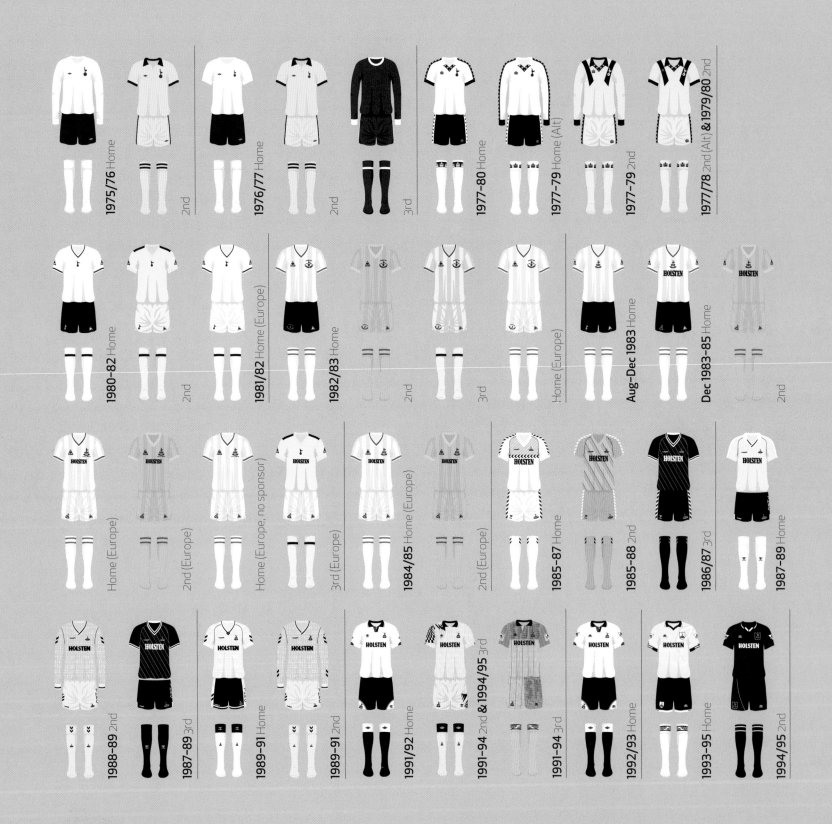

1975/76 Home

2nd

1976/77 Home

2nd

3rd

1977–80 Home

1977–79 Home (Alt)

1977–79 2nd

1977/78 2nd (Alt) & 1979/80 2nd

1980–82 Home

2nd

1981/82 Home (Europe)

1982/83 Home

2nd

3rd

Home (Europe)

Aug–Dec 1983 Home

Dec 1983–85 Home

2nd

Home (Europe)

2nd (Europe)

Home (Europe, no sponsor)

3rd (Europe)

1984/85 Home (Europe)

2nd (Europe)

1985–87 Home

1985–88 2nd

1986/87 3rd

1987–89 Home

1988–89 2nd

1987–89 3rd

1989–91 Home

1989–91 2nd

1991/92 Home

1991–94 2nd & 1994/95 3rd

1991–94 3rd

1992/93 Home

1993–95 Home

1994/95 2nd

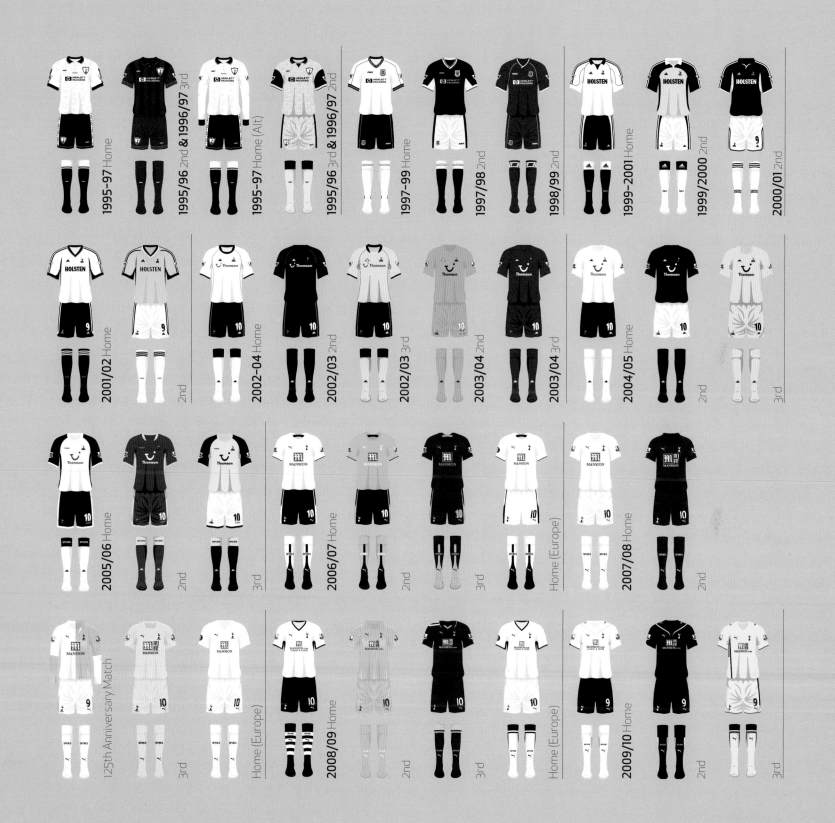

1995–97 Home

1995/96 2nd & 1996/97 3rd

1995–97 Home (Alt)

1995/96 3rd & 1996/97 2nd

1997–99 Home

1997/98 2nd

1998/99 2nd

1999–2001 Home

1999/2000 2nd

2000/01 2nd

2001/02 Home

2nd

2002–04 Home

2002/03 2nd

2002/03 3rd

2003/04 2nd

2003/04 3rd

2004/05 Home

2nd

3rd

2005/06 Home

2nd

3rd

2006/07 Home

2nd

3rd

Home (Europe)

2007/08 Home

2nd

125th Anniversary Match

3rd

Home (Europe)

2008/09 Home

2nd

3rd

Home (Europe)

2009/10 Home

2nd

3rd

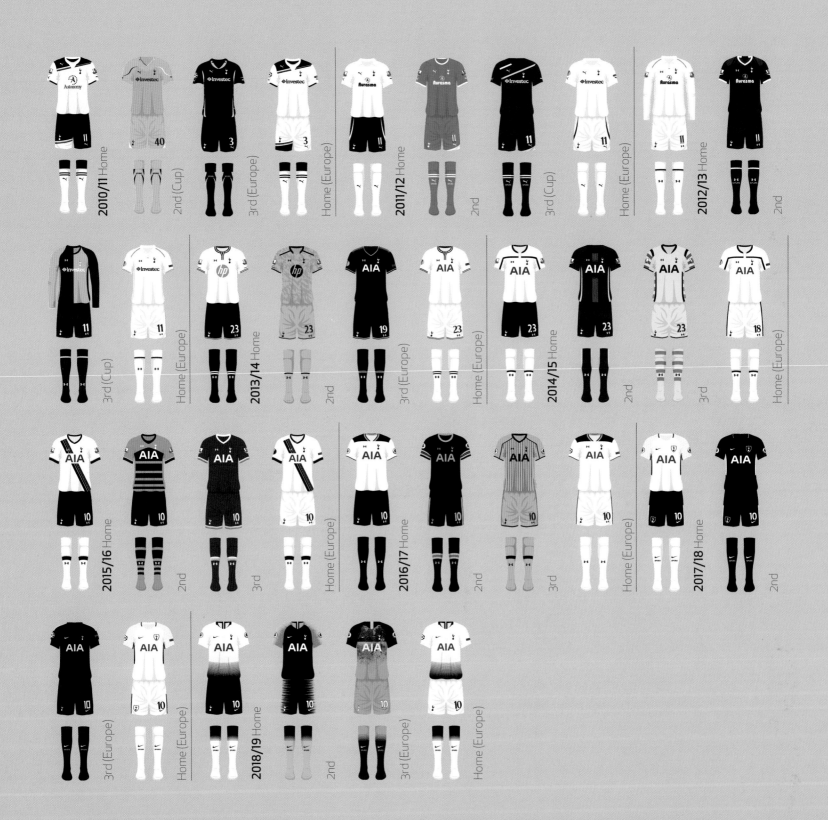

2010/11 Home

2nd (Cup)

3rd (Europe)

Home (Europe)

2011/12 Home

2nd

3rd (Cup)

Home (Europe)

2012/13 Home

2nd

3rd (Cup)

Home (Europe)

2013/14 Home

2nd

3rd (Europe)

Home (Europe)

2014/15 Home

2nd

3rd

Home (Europe)

2015/16 Home

2nd

3rd

Home (Europe)

2016/17 Home

2nd

3rd

Home (Europe)

2017/18 Home

2nd

3rd (Europe)

Home (Europe)

2018/19 Home

2nd

3rd (Europe)

Home (Europe)

# CUP FINAL KITS

The complete record of the exact kits worn in all the major cup finals in which Tottenham Hotspur Football Club has appeared

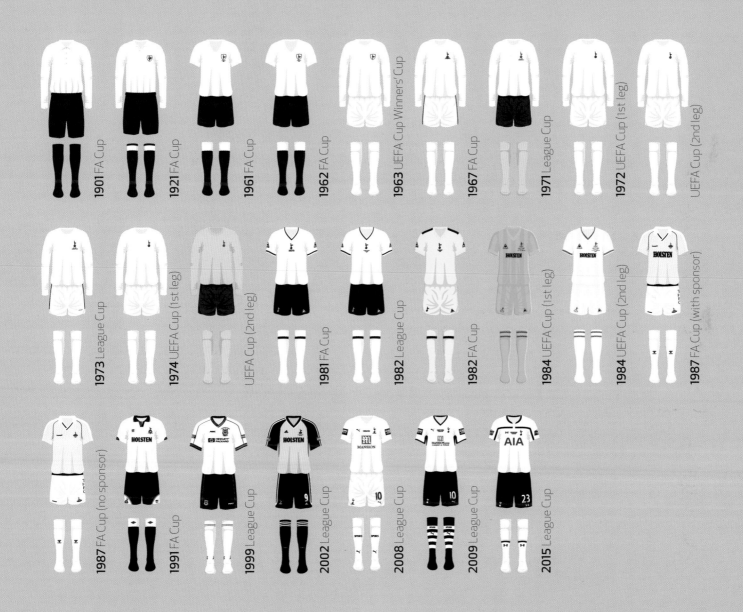

1901 FA Cup

1921 FA Cup

1961 FA Cup

1962 FA Cup

1963 UEFA Cup Winners' Cup

1967 FA Cup

1971 League Cup

1972 UEFA Cup (1st leg)

UEFA Cup (2nd leg)

1973 League Cup

1974 UEFA Cup (1st leg)

UEFA Cup (2nd leg)

1981 FA Cup

1982 League Cup

1982 FA Cup

1984 UEFA Cup (1st leg)

1984 UEFA Cup (2nd leg)

1987 FA Cup (with sponsor)

1987 FA Cup (no sponsor)

1991 FA Cup

1999 League Cup

2002 League Cup

2008 League Cup

2009 League Cup

2015 League Cup

# ACKNOWLEDGEMENTS

All three authors would like to thank the following former Tottenham Hotspur players and managers for their time and priceless insight: Steve Perryman, Ossie Ardiles, Phil Beal, Keith Burkinshaw, Martin Chivers, Terry Dyson, Justin Edinburgh, Tony Galvin, Ricky George, Alan Gilzean, Richard Gough, Micky Hazard, Cliff Jones, Ledley King, Gary Mabbutt, Paul Miller, Tony Parks, Graham Roberts, Steve Sedgley, Paul Stewart, Gary Stevens, Martin Thomas and Ricky Villa, as well as irrepressible laundry lady Sylvie Webb.

Special thanks, too, to former members of staff at the club, as well as current Tottenham Hotspur Football Club employees: Jamey Bashford, Julie Bracey, John Fennelly, Gary Jacobson, Victoria Hawksley, Jon Rayner, Mike Rollo and Cindy Wolf.

The majority of the shirts included in this book have come from the personal collections of two of the authors, Daren and Neville, but a huge thank you must also go to the following collectors who have all allowed shirts from their collections to be included: Colin Webb, Robert Segal, John Bowers, Darren Eckersley, Robert Hall, Ian Langley, Mario Sartori, Jeff Maysh, Nick Sion and Nigel Wray. The authors would also especially like to acknowledge the massively significant contribution of Liam Ridley, not only for the shirts from his impressive collection but his in-depth knowledge of the history of match worn Spurs shirts.

In addition, the following provided invaluable insider insight: Simon Bamber, 'Pudsey' Bevan, Robbie Brightwell, Bobby Brown, Dave Holmes, Aaron Lavery, John Metselaar, Bert Patrick, Bill Perryman, Bob Roberts and Kevin Batchelor.

The authors would also like to thank the following for sharing their historical knowledge: John Devlin, Lee Hermitage, Glen Isherwood, Dave Moor, Eugenio Palopoli, Rob Sawyer, the first of our kit researchers Andy Rockall, illustrator Daniel Gellatley, and our good friends Gavin Haigh, Neal Heard, Ronnie Kidd, Rob Stokes, Andy Tasker and Denis Hurley, whose wealth of knowledge never ceased to amaze us. A huge thanks is also due to our other researcher, Tony Sealey, who is the oracle of Tottenham Hotspur kit history and whose input to this book has been priceless.

Many thanks also to Spurs historian Bob Goodwin for his invaluable assistance on the historical side of things, and to the family of the late Andy Porter for allowing access to his collection.

On the photography side of things, thank you to Mansel Davies and Malcolm Jenkins for the Wales photoshoot, Alex Jackson and Tim Ashmore of The National Football Museum, and the master, Paul Downes, and the excellent Lee Murrells, Aneta Swoboda and Emma Morton at 3Objectives Photography.

The authors would also like to thank our publishers, the Vision Sports Publishing crew of Toby Trotman, Ulrika Drewett, Paul Baillie-Lane, Ed Davis, and our writer Adam Powley.

But a very special thanks and appreciation, particularly from Simon, to the book's editor Jim Drewett and designer Doug Cheeseman for their patience, their belief in the project and, most of all, for sticking with it.

We sincerely apologise to anybody else we may have forgotten.

## PICTURE CREDITS

All shirt photography by Paul Downes at 3Objectives Photography and Mansel Davies Photography.

Getty Images: 6-7, 8, 9, 11, 12, 14, 16, 19, 27, 28, 31, 34, 38, 40, 42, 44, 46-47, 52, 56, 58, 66, 68, 72, 76, 83(2), 85(2), 87, 88, 89, 90, 92, 96, 98, 100, 104, 106, 107, 108, 110, 116, 120, 122, 135, 136, 137, 140, 142, 144, 149, 152, 166, 172, 176, 178, 180, 186, 188, 190, 192, 194, 195, 196, 198, 200, 205, 206, 208, 209, 211, 218, 224, 228, 232, 236, 241(2), 244, 246, 250, 252, 256, 258, 264, 268, 269, 280, 284, 288, 292, 294, 298, 302, 304, 308, 312, 315, 319, 320, 321(3), 322, 326
PA Photos: 48, 49, 62, 64, 84, 102, 146, 148, 152, 174, 182, 194, 195, 205, 212, 307; Colorsport: 10, 16-17, 22, 29, 32, 60, 70, 80-81, 118, 132, 202, 306; Action Images: 15, 156, 158, 168, 170, 184, 262, 315; Tim Reder: 274-275 (2), 276-277; Nike: 13, 17, 319-19; Mirrorpix: 54, 114, 130; Offside: 112, 160, 309; National Football Museum: 164, 165; Alamy: 128; Andy Hooper: 23; Bobby Buckle Family Collection: 25; Nigel Wray/National Football Museum: 41(2)

Memorabilia and historical material from the collections of Tottenham Hotspur Football Club, Bob Goodwin, Neville Evans and the late Andy Porter. Every effort has been made to contact the copyright holders of the photographs used in this book. If there are any errors or omissions the publishers will be pleased to receive information.

## ABOUT THE AUTHORS

### Simon 'Shakey' Shakeshaft

A highly respected match worn shirt collector of nearly 30 years, Simon is the curator of The Neville Evans National Football Shirt Collection and works with a number of UK auction houses on player shirt authentication. 'Shakey' is a previously published author on the subject of football shirt history and regularly contributes to a number of other publications and media outlets on the subject of match worn shirts.

### Daren Burney

Daren has been an avid Spurs supporter for more than 40 years since his first White Hart Lane visit in September 1976. He has been an associate director at Tottenham Hotspur Football Club since 2007, during which time he has worked on Land Assembly for the New Stadium Project and Area Regeneration. For Daren, working on this book represents a dream come true after a lifetime of collecting Tottenham Hotspur memorabilia.

### Neville Evans

A lifelong Tottenham Hotspur supporter and an ardent collector of football memorabilia since the 1990s, Neville is the owner of the largest football collection in private ownership in the UK, which includes The National Football Collection and The National Football Shirt Collection. Neville has many items on display at The National Football Museum and regularly loans items to other museums and exhibitions around the world.

This book is dedicated to all the ladies in the authors' lives:

*From Simon to Tracey, Georgia and Coco*

*From Daren to Paula, Hannah, Sarah and Chloe*

*And from Neville to Susan, Courtney and Kelsey*

*Thank you for your love, encouragement and support all throughout this project.*